**Max Bill's
View of Things**

Max Bill's View of Things
Die gute Form: An Exhibition 1949

Edited by Lars Müller
in collaboration with
the Museum für Gestaltung Zürich

With texts by
Jakob Bill
Max Bill
Claude Lichtenstein
Renate Menzi
Deyan Sudjic

Lars Müller Publishers

The entrance area designed by Max Bill for the Basel exhibition in May 1949.
The white panel, incorporating the plinth for the sculpture *rhythm in space*
(1947–48), covered the bland entrance to the sports hall at the Mustermesse site.

9	**When we knew what good design was**
	Deyan Sudjic
19	**The appealing design of the good object**
	Claude Lichtenstein
39	***Die gute Form* display panels**
41	Forms in nature, science, art and technology
57	Forms in planning and architecture
75	Forms in home fittings and furnishings
107	Forms in various appliances and modes of transportation
124	***die gute form*—good design also as a configuration of panels**
	jakob bill
143	**beauty from function and as function**
	max bill
146	**good form**
	max bill
148	**the conditions of work over the period of *die gute form***
	jakob bill
152	Chronology
155	**Around the world in eighty plates**
	Renate Menzi
158	Biography

When we knew what good design was
Deyan Sudjic

When Kathryn Hiesinger organized *Design Since 1945,* an exhibition that opened at the Philadelphia Museum of Art in 1983, she invited both Ettore Sottsass and Max Bill to answer the same five questions and printed their responses in the catalog. The first question was: "What are the qualities of good design?" Bill used just sixteen words to answer it. Sottsass needed all of three sentences.

Bill was more expansive in 1949 with his exhibition *Die gute Form.* He began by nailing his colors to the mast, with a selection of images of naturally occurring forms, such as crystals and polarized lights. Disturbingly, a mushroom cloud is shown alongside dyes floating languidly in water, diffraction rings, molecules, and hydrocarbons seen through an electron microscope, followed by a selection of mathematically generated forms. Evidently, for Bill, the starting point for good design is the kind of beauty that comes in the shape of ideal forms, which are to be found through the exploration of nature, and rational logic. The exhibition followed this with a series of typologies of varying scales: industrial equipment, bridges, city plans, architecture, furniture, automobiles, aircraft, interiors, and clothes. This range of scales and categories is another reflection of Bill's attitudes: his version perhaps of Ernesto Rogers's concept of the architect's role as stretching from the spoon to the city.

However, Bill gave fashion short shrift. For him, it appeared that garments meant nothing more than protective clothing: there are rain hats, waterproof wind jackets, sandals, and ski boots. Adolf Loos took a more nuanced view of fashion, a subject that interested him in a way that it seems not to have touched Bill. His exhibition moves on through toys, top-loading washing machines, the seemingly anonymous Oskar Rüegg corkscrew, cheese graters, and a British prefab house. You somehow expect Bill to have selected electricity pylons and Robert Maillart bridges for inclusion, and you find them in abundance. But unexpectedly you also find the Rockefeller Center, a complex on the edge of Art Deco—a style that is the antithesis of Bill's forensic approach to form.

Bill was modest about showing his own work in the exhibition, but not so modest as to exclude it altogether. There is a sculpture of his alongside works by Naum Gabo, Georges Vantongerloo, Constantin Brancusi, Jean Arp, and Antoine Pevsner. A typewriter that he designed for the long-vanished Swiss brand Birchmeier is shown next to one of Marcello Nizzoli's less impressive works for Olivetti. And he put his spun aluminum light shade next to Isamu Noguchi's three-legged cylinder paper lamp, though with a notable lack of Swiss thoroughness managed to spell it "Naguchi."

Italy hardly figures in Bill's universe even though he had spent time in Milan and met Sottsass by the time of the exhibition. He shows a couple of projects by Marcello Nizzoli, a Cisitalia automobile by Pininfarina—as seen in the Museum of Modern Art's permanent collection—and a Pier Luigi Nervi concrete shell next to Giò Ponti's very unrationalist coffeemaker for La Pavoni.

Bill is surprisingly unpredictable. Yes, there is a Hans Coray aluminum chair and an Eero Saarinen womb chair. But for a figure with a reputation of being a chilly rationalist, there is a surprising number of works by Charlotte Perriand in her Japanese period. I would not have expected Bill to be an enthusiast for Frank Lloyd Wright, but in fact he selected Johnson Wax, Florida Southern College's chapel, and Taliesin West. And the other two architects who get top billing are Richard Neutra and Alvar Aalto, with nothing from Hannes Meyer—perhaps suggesting that something untoward passed between the two of them in the year and a half that they overlapped at the Bauhaus in Dessau. Nor is there anything from Braun: it was too soon for Dieter Rams to have made a mark. Instead there was Kobler's dangerous-looking electric shaver, a cigarette holder, the Hilba camera, and the Murphy radio—all of them destined for obscurity.

To judge by the large number of technical objects, such as substations from Brown Boveri, the Carrosserie Graber cabriolet on a Rover chassis, and the British Gloster Meteor jet, some of what appealed to Bill would turn out to be anything but timeless. On the other hand, he identified such fascinating but little-known pioneering work as William Pereira's Tuberculosis sanatorium in Waukegan from 1938, housing by Emil Roth, Alfred Roth, and Marcel Breuer in Zurich, a very early folding table designed by Charles Eames that never went into mass production, and a ring by Harry Bertoia. It is a selection that shows impressive sensibility as well as tireless curiosity. Taken as a whole, it represents a powerful and persuasive visual argument.

The idea of "good design" (*gute Form*), has continued to resonate over the decades. Even now in our own relativist times, when no museum of design is comfortable with accepting the role of a pantheon containing nothing but examples of good design, when design is expected to ask questions rather than answer them, and when design endorsements from organizations such as Red Dot have become straightforward commercial transactions, the idea that there might be such a thing as good design continues to provide a faint background hum to the discussion. The concept of good and therefore also of bad design has been deeply ingrained into our thinking and our perception. It draws on the idea that a close enough study of the functional requirements of a category of objects or buildings will produce the best possible functional solution to the problem. This solution, it is believed, is one that will at the same time represent something that is also beautiful. In fact this is not a technical issue, but a philosophical one. At a poetic level, the functionalist ideal recalls these lines in John Keats's "Ode on a Grecian Urn": "Beauty is truth, truth beauty—that is all / Ye know on earth, and all ye need to know." His words are a reminder that the functional ideal may be more aesthetic than utilitarian. And to suggest that there can be "truth" to materials is to suggest that there is a moral virtue to "good" design.

There is no question that this was also *Max Bill's View of Things.* He was suggesting that good design was a kind of crusade. So did Sir Henry Cole, the guiding genius of the Great Exhibition in London of 1851 and the force behind the establishment of the Victoria and Albert Museum. Cole set up a display that was meant to demonstrate to the general public, to students, and to manufacturers, precisely what constituted good design. Alongside it was a demonstration of what Cole believed to be bad design. This display was called *Examples of False Principles in Decoration* and dubbed the "Chamber of Horrors" by Cole's critics. In an echo of Cole, Stephen Bayley, director of the precursor to London's Design Museum, the Boilerhouse exhibition space at the Victoria and Albert Museum, staged a show there titled *Taste* in the 1980s. Bayley placed objects whose design he saw as valuable on easels whereas others were impaled on dustbins.

The Council of Industrial Design was established in 1944 under the leadership of Gordon Russell, a designer and manufacturer of furniture, who represented the last gasp of the Arts and Crafts tradition. It later became the Design Council and staged the morale-boosting exhibition *Britain Can Make It* at the Victoria and Albert Museum in 1946, just before Bill's exhibition. It filled the entire museum before its permanent collections, which had been evacuated during the war, were brought back to London. These were exhibits based on new designs from British manufacturers that were aimed for the export markets, alongside experiments with new materials, and with new typologies. On the crest of this wave, the Council of Industrial Design established *Design* magazine in 1949, a publication dedicated to the same mission of preaching the gospel of good design. In its pages it seemed that nothing had changed since Henry Cole's chamber of horrors. A century later *Design*'s editors were still railing against wheat sheaf ornament applied to the sides of electric pop-up toasters. Russell, the Council's first leader, asked: "What do we mean by good design? First, does it exist? It is often said that there is no such thing as good design or bad design, that design has no real measurable standards, that it is just a measure of personal taste; that because an article sells in great quantities, this alone proves it must be well designed"— apparently taking a swipe at Raymond Loewy and his famous *TIME Magazine* cover as the man who "streamlines the sales curve."

Much the same things were being said in New York, where Eliot Noyes was appointed the first head of the newly formed department of design at the Museum of Modern Art in 1940. Like Max Bill, Noyes had been taught by serval Bauhaus professors, although in his case it was at Harvard rather than in Dessau. Noyes, briefly Marcel Breuer's partner, wrote that "good design in everyday objects shows the taste and good sense of the designers. On none is there arbitrarily applied decoration […] These things really look like what they are." While he was at the Museum of Modern Art Noyes curated *Useful Objects of American Design under $10,* an exhibition in which he set out to demonstrate that America was full of good, anonymous design, showing objects that he discovered in hardware stores and office supply companies. He followed this in 1944 with *Design for Use,* when he suggested that "A good design should have nothing which is irrelevant, accidental, or unrelated to the main idea. It is discouraging to see how many automobiles this year have been disfigured by cheap tricks. The most obvious is the undisciplined use of chrome. Bright metal accents can certainly be used when related to the whole design with care and thoughtfulness. As used on a number of cars, they are trashy, and when some of the two-tone color schemes are added, they are worse. There are many other offensive little details. For example the little portholes on the side of the Buick are dead-end plugs—pseudo-utilitarian decoration. The charitable thought strikes one that perhaps the sales department forced these gimmicks down the throats of reluctant and unhappy designers, and that even General Motors could produce a work of art if freed from such compulsions."

Noyes left to work for IBM, but his successor at the Museum of Modern Art, Edgar Kaufmann, was just as dismissive of the American approach to industrial design, as represented by Loewy, Norman Bel Geddes, and Henry Dreyfuss. "A frequent misconception is that the principal purpose of good modern design is to facilitate trade and that big sales are proof of excellence in design. Not so. Sales are episodes in the careers of designed objects. Use is the first consideration." An exhibition that Noyes curated at Yale while teaching there was titled *Modern Design, the Search for Appropriate Form.* It included what was described as "a room of well-designed objects" alongside a display of vernacular, anonymous objects to suggest that "appropriate form often develops naturally." The exhibition comprised the following manifesto:

Good Design
1 Fulfills its function
2 Respects its materials
3 Is suited to the method of production
4 Combines these in imaginative expression

It is a formulation that closely reflects Bill's selection.

In her exhibition in Philadelphia, Hiesinger was attempting to demonstrate the polar opposites in postwar design. In 1983 Sottsass had just established the Memphis Group. For Bill, who had been the cofounder of what he hoped would be the natural successor of the Bauhaus, the Ulm School of Design seemed like its antithesis. As Hiesinger pointed out, both of them were painters and architects, as well as designers, polemicists, and writers. Despite all appearances to the contrary, Sottsass and Bill had once been closer in their attitudes than the disjunctive caricature of playful anarchy set against sober rectitude might have suggested. Sottsass had met Bill for the first time at *Arte astratta e concreta,* the exhibition that opened in Milan's Palazzo Reale in January 1947. It was the launch of the Movimento per l'arte concreta (MAC). A decade later, when he was at Olivetti, Sottsass's first two employees were both Ulm graduates. Tomas Maldonado, Bill's onetime protégé, who was later to become his bête noire at the school, led the research project on which the keyboard for the Tekne 3 typewriter designed by Sottsass was based.

By 1983 Bill and Sottsass were philosophically far enough apart for Hiesinger's stratagem to succeed perfectly. Bill's answer to Hiesinger's question was satisfyingly brusque. "Good design depends on the harmony established between the form of an object and its use." Sottsass was equally satisfyingly subversive. "This is a question that supposes a Platonic view of the situation, that is, it supposes that somewhere, somehow, there is a place where GOOD DESIGN is deposited. The problem then is to come as close as possible to that 'good design.' My idea instead is that the problem is not to be near 'good design' but to design, keeping as near as possible to the anthropological state of things, which, in turn, is to be as near as possible to the need a society has for an image of itself." Hiesinger's second question was to ask how these values endured in the face of technology. Bill replied that "technological changes should help to make the object better and more harmonious in form and in function, as well as cheaper." Sottsass responded: "They don't endure at all, because in my definition the qualities of good design are exactly the ones that don't endure but follow the changes of history, the changes of the anthropological state of things. And among them, the changes of technology. If you really want to find something that endures, that is the intensity of the research for a relationship between history, and a possible image of history. In design what endures is man's curiosity toward existence, and the drive to give a metaphoric image to it."

It is the special quality of design that it is constantly shifting and adjusting its nature. Good design is a period piece. Design is constantly relevant, constantly fascinating. And in that, Sottsass's answer was perhaps fuller and subtler than Bill's, yet for all that there are aspects of Bill's exhibition that continue to project a poignantly effective reflection of a world in which our aesthetic choices seemed so much clearer than they are now, a world for whose loss we cannot but feel regret.

Deyan Sudjic is an architectural and design theoretician and director of the Design Museum, London.

Exhibition visitors, display panels, and some of the furniture selected by Bill: a laminated wood chair by Horgen-Glarus, a Landi garden chair by Hans Coray, Indi lamp by Sigfried Giedion and Hin Bredendieck, and a Strub shelf and "colonial chair" by Wilhelm Kienzle.

The appealing design of the good object
Claude Lichtenstein

The 80 display panels mounted on slender roof-batten uprights and the few objects—furniture, lighting, appliances, and objects—that were on show at *Die gute Form,* the special exhibition held as part of the 1949 Basel Mustermesse trade fair, had a far-reaching impact on the history of design and everyday culture. On each panel, three objects were presented in the form of black-and-white photographs accompanied by a brief caption that drew attention to the distinctive design features and quality of each product—a total of 240 examples ranging from women's shoes to electricity pylons and from an army jeep to a flower vase. The panels were intended to convey to manufacturers and the public the importance of the coherent design of manually and industrially produced goods. Up to that point, the formal aesthetics of, for example, household objects, lighting, and rolling stock had been discussed only within small circles of professional designers. The exhibition now became the harbinger of a new attitude toward life that would find expression in particular in the modern design of capital and consumer goods.

The special exhibition, which lasted ten days, formed the prelude to two touring exhibitions that were conceived and produced by Max Bill on behalf of the Swiss Werkbund (SWB). The "Swiss" version started in Basel and subsequently visited a number of other cities in Switzerland, before traveling on to Austria and the Netherlands, while the "German" version was already touring Germany by the end of May 1949; both attracted great attention everywhere they went.[1] (In summer 1949 the idea of creating a third, English-language version for Great Britain and Scandinavia was considered, but never implemented.) Outside Switzerland, the exhibition encountered a post-war milieu completely different to unspoiled Basel: mountains of rubble that had not yet been cleared away, yawning gaps in the cityscape, shortages, and shame, anger, grief, and defiance.[2]

Die gute Form inspired a whole series of institutionalized and groundbreaking bodies and events that served to spotlight and popularize the design quality of objects through the award of prizes for good design. These prizes included, in Switzerland, Die gute Form SWB, introduced in 1951 and awarded up 1968, in Italy the Premio Compasso d'Oro (as from 1954), and in Germany the rating Die gute Industrieform granted by the Verein Industrieform (as from 1954) and the Bundespreis Gute Form. By no means all of this met with Bill's approval—as we shall see later on. What is certain, however, is that Bill had read the signs of the times and became one of the first in Europe after 1945 to revive the discussion of the design quality of everyday objects.[3] In contrast to the 1920s, when the debate had revolved primarily around the aesthetics of form,

[1] See "die gute form—good design also as a configuration of panels" by Jakob Bill, pp. 124–31.

[2] The fact that many families who had been forced or bombed out of their homes missed their former surroundings and longed to recreate them was perceived as a problem by those interested in the future of design in Germany. They wanted to put a stop to the trend in nostalgic shoddy goods that industry was supplying to this market.

[3] In as early as 1946 Bill published his essay "Erfahrungen bei der Formgestaltung von Industrieprodukten," in: *Werk* 5 (1946), pp. 167–70. With this issue the journal *Werk* began differentiating for the first time between the categories of "industrial arts" (*Kunstgewerbe*) and "industrial design" (*Industrielle Formgebung*).

technical manufacturing and economic issues and their impact on design quality were now much more important. In a way that is difficult to quantify, *Die gute Form* was part cause, part effect and part symptom of this new preoccupation with good design, something that becomes all the clearer when we take the international context into account.[4]

The Museum of Modern Art in New York had been organizing exhibitions under the title *Useful Objects* since 1938, and in November 1950 opened its first exhibition under the title *Good Design*.[5] Inspired by the Merchandise Mart in Chicago, the show was devoted to furniture and living accessories (criteria: "Eye appeal, function, construction, and price, with emphasis on the first").[6] For MoMA, it marked the first in a long series of exhibitions with this title. Did this change of name—from *Useful Objects* (1938–1947) to *Good Design*—mark a change of emphasis and did this, in turn, have something to do with *Die gute Form*? The timing of the change is certainly striking. There is no doubt that *Die gute Form* prompted the creation of the Compasso d'Oro in Italy. This award, which had a major influence upon the development of Italian post-war design, was launched by the Milan department store La Rinascente, where the graphic designer Max Huber—already a friend of Bill—was employed in the advertising department. At the end of 1949, the Union des artistes modernes (UAM) in France mounted the exhibition *Formes utiles,* in which Bill was invited by René Herbst to take part.[7]

For the media-savvy Max Bill, *Die gute Form* fell into the years in which he made his international breakthrough as an artist, designer, and theoretician. Immediately after the war he gave a number of well-received talks in Germany on the subject of reconstruction. In 1949 he published his book on Robert Maillart, the Swiss civil engineer, bridge constructor, and pioneer of structural reinforced concrete. The following year he was invited to São Paulo, where the Museo d'Arte Moderna held the first major retrospective of his painting and sculptures and where he was subsequently awarded the Grand Prix for sculpture at the 1951 São Paulo Bienal. During this same period, Bill played a key role in the creation of the Hochschule für Gestaltung in Ulm. He changed its planned orientation as a school of political culture to that of a school of design, drew up the plans for its campus—his most important work of architecture—and in 1953 became its first rector.[8]

The path of events leading up to the exhibition *Die gute Form* was not entirely smooth. (See also the overview on p. 152–53.) Its earliest origins can be traced back to the 1947 Milan Triennale, when Bill was considered

4 It is important to distinguish between the special/touring exhibition *Die gute Form* and the prize of the same name (Die gute Form SWB) that it inspired. This prize was awarded for the first time in 1952 and subsequently annually up to 1968. (The award was officially abolished in 1969.) As the initial spark for the annual award, too, the special exhibition propelled the Swiss Werkbund to a position of great respect and influence. See Peter Erni, *Die gute Form: Eine Aktion des Schweizerischen Werkbundes. Dokumentation and Interpretationen* (Baden, 1983).

5 The exhibition ran from Nov. 21, 1950 to Jan. 28, 1951. See also Arthur Pulos, *The American Design Adventure. 1940–1975* (Boston, 1988), p. 111. (NB The dates given by Pulos are inaccurate.)

6 Source MoMA archives: "Useful Objects Exhibit," Internet search of May 6, 2013: www.moma.org./learn/resources/archives/archives_exhibition_history_list See also Pulos, p. 110.

7 On Feb. 26, 1949 Bill wrote a letter regarding *Die gute Form* to Herbst. The latter's reply of Mar. 18, 1949 also contains a reference to the planned exhibition *Formes utiles*. Herbst's invitation to Bill to take part in *Formes utiles* followed on July 11, 1949 (max, binia + jakob bill foundation, adligenswil).

8 The Hochschule für Gestaltung was originally going to be called the Geschwister Scholl Hochschule after its founders, Inge Scholl and Otl Aicher, and was conceived as a college for democratically minded politicians and media professionals as a step toward repairing the intellectual damage caused by National Socialism. The reorientation of its teaching program and its renaming as the Hochschule für Gestaltung both went back to suggestions by Bill.

by the fair management for the design of the entrance hall; although the commission never materialized, it nevertheless started him on the trail of thought leading to *Die gute Form*.[9]

In winter 1947/48 the SWB planned an "educational touring exhibition" for Switzerland and abroad.[10] In April 1948 Bill submitted his proposal for an exhibition to be titled "zweck + konstruktion = form" (purpose + construction = design). It was to consist of four sections, each comprising 22 panels and with the following headings: 1. Design clearly demonstrating function; 2. Design in architecture; 3. Design in the home; 4. Design in daily life. (The copy in the Design Collection at the ZHdK carries the handwritten note "sample panels in ca. 14 days.")[11] This established the format from which *Die gute Form* evolved. Bill set out the aims for the project in a few short words: "this touring exhibition aims to provide an insight, in particular in other German-speaking countries, into the problems of functional design and thereby to inform as wide an audience as possible about the results achieved to date and their foundations. through the way in which it is presented, the exhibition is intended not only to address directly interested parties such as producers and consumers, but also, and above all, to offer basic material aimed at the education of the next generation of designers and the further education of designers already practising."[12]

At the end of October 1948 the Swiss Werkbund held a conference in Basel on the relationship between design and the economy. The director of the Mustermesse trade fair, Theodor Brogle, spoke on the subject of "The notion of quality and design in Swiss industry" and Bill gave his much-discussed talk on "Beauty from function and as function."[13] (see pp. 143–45). By this point in time, the idea of mounting the planned exhibition in the context of industrial manufacturing had already been formulated.

The exhibition itself had to be organized in just a few weeks, since the financing was only put in place two months before the opening. It proved difficult to convince the minister responsible, Federal Councillor Philipp Etter, of the increasing importance to the national economy of well-designed industrial products.[14] In the funding application that the SWB submitted to the federal state government in January 1949, the title of the exhibition was changed to "Funktion und Form."[15] It is evident that Bill's original title had triggered a certain amount of discussion, and even more so that Bill himself, as he pursued the topic more intensively, had begun to see things differently and no longer considered his original suggestion appropriate. I shall return to this below.

9 Letter from Egidius Streiff/SWB to Pro Helvetia, Feb. 12, 1948 (ZHdK/MfGZ/DS/Konvolut SWB). See also Roberto Fabbri, *Max Bill in Italia—Lo spazio logico dell'architettura,* (Milan 2011), chap. "La Triennale mancata," pp. 49ff.

10 The SWB exhibition committee consisted of Alfred Altherr, Werner Bischof, Max Bill, Hans Finsler, Alfred Roth, Egidius Streiff and B. von Grünigen (ZHdK/MfGZ/DS/Konvolut SWB).

11 Max Bill, "exposé für eine wanderausstellung" (ibid.).

12 Altherr, minutes of the 4th 1950 meeting of the SWB exhibition committee, Oct. 11, 1950.

13 The conference took place on October 23/24, 1948, with the lectures delivered on October 23. ("Protokoll der Generalversammlung 1948 des Schweizerischen Werkbundes im Kunstmuseum Basel," SWB Archives, Zurich office.) See Max Bill, "Schönheit aus Funktion and als Funktion," in *Werk*, 8 (1949), pp. 272ff. For an English translation of this lecture, see pp. 143–45.

14 Letter of Dec. 18, 1948 (ZHdK/MfGZ/DS/Konvolut SWB). Consent of the minister responsible, Federal Councillor Philipp Etter, granted on Mar. 18, 1949 (ibid.). On March 24 Pro Helvetia retracted the money it had provisionally awarded—CHF 6,000—and demanded that only appliances should be shown on the panels and that the examples of architecture should be dropped, "since two exhibitions on architecture have already been shown in Germany. We don't want to give the impression abroad that Switzerland has nothing to show but architecture." Bill was able to overcome this new obstacle with his explanatory reply of Mar. 28, 1949 (ibid.).

15 Letter of Jan. 13, 1949 (ibid.).

The appealing design of the good object

It is unlikely that Bill did nothing on the project between October 1948 and February 1949. We can assume that he spent these months forming a clearer picture of the selection of objects to be shown, matching suitable examples to the panels he had in mind, and optimistically commissioning images (e.g. from photographers and fellow Werkbund members Werner Bischof, Hans Finsler, Ernst Heiniger, and Hugo P. Herdeg). A bulging file of correspondence held by the max, binia + jakob bill foundation contains copies of letter from Bill and the replies he received.[16] On February 25, 1949 Bill sent out a first round of letters to various addressees in the US and Great Britain, in which he requested borderless prints of the objects he wanted to show, in good quality, measuring 24 × 30 cm, and in triplicate. One letter went to the Department of Architectural & Industrial Design at the Museum of Modern Art in New York. Here Bill asked for the names and addresses of American designers. Curator Peter Blake promptly replied with a list of individuals whom Bill immediately contacted.[17] This approach via MoMA was a matter of tacit agreement and meant that Bill did not lose valuable time sending requests to unsuitable designers.

The 80 panels produced under such time pressure probably represent a mixture of Bill's own favorites, items he found in journals and perhaps also recommendations by third parties. Behind them, invisible, are the contacts that never materialized, the enquiries to which Bill received no replies, and the documents delivered too late for inclusion. Bill wrote two unanswered letters to the designer Raymond Loewy, for example, regarding the latter's Parker fountain pen,[18] while the photograph that he had requested of the first Porsche sports car did not arrive in time.

The reactions to Bill's enquiries ranged from enthusiastic agreement to curt refusals. It is today hard to credit the standoffishness of a global company such as Escher Wyss, who could not see the point of the thing and only grudgingly supplied the photographs requested.[19] Despite all these difficulties, Bill managed to get the exhibition together on time. He grouped the material under four main headings and presented the display panels in correspondingly distinct areas:
1 Forms in nature, science, art and technology
2 Forms in planning and architecture
3 Forms in home fittings and furnishings
4 Forms in various appliances and modes of transportation

These divisions were basically the same as in the original concept; the only difference was in the number of panels, since the categories were no longer all the same size, as initially planned. So that visitors would be

16 "die gute form" file held in the max, binia + jakob bill foundation, adligenswil. (in the following: m., b. + j. b. f.)

17 This correspondence was conducted by airmail, with the corresponding delays.

18 max, binia + jakob bill foundation, adligenswil. For his book *Form*, Bill subsequently chose Loewy's Hallicrafters radio receiver.

19 They also made a fuss about a token contribution to costs (just a few francs) that was not even compulsory (m., b. + j. b. f.).

able to see exactly where one section ended and the next began, Bill designed a serpentine layout that wound through the middle of the exhibition space and used the switch from convex to concave curve to mark the boundary between topics. He thereby created an unusually active and autonomous arrangement that was very different to the wall-hung style of presentation conventionally employed up to that date.[20] With this display concept, which was employed in all the stops along the tour, he created a core element that compensated for the heterogeneity of the different locations.

The exhibition in Basel was well attended and met with much approval from the public and press. Reviews in the media were friendly and favorable, but also somewhat naive and superficial.[21] The press photo of the opening shows Bill in front of the entrance (specially built for the exhibition) with his sculpture, handing out exhibition guides to arriving visitors. In the printed guide, he explains what the idea of good design and a good form means:
We understand "good design" to mean a natural form for a product developed out of its functional and technical requirements and which fulfills the intended purpose in a visually appealing way. The examples shown here were selected according to these criteria.[22]

Ernst Scheidegger's photographs of the interior of the hall convey a good impression of the exhibition layout and give a sense, too, of how the public may have reacted to its examples of "good design"—depending on the panel, with astonishment or amazement, irritation or fascination, approval or disapproval, or simply amusement. Whatever the case, *Die gute Form* undoubtedly offered many new ideas and much food for thought (see fig. 16, 17).[23]

Within the SWB, there was much criticism of the exhibition after it was over, even taking into account the difficult circumstances in which it arose. In the verdict of the local Basel branch of the SWB: "It did not fulfill its purpose of winning support for our aims from large strata of the trade fair visitors […] The objects on display represent just one direction within the Werkbund's endeavors. […] The photographs show a disproportionately large number of foreign products, with too little space granted to Swiss products and none at all to those by our local group. […] Major areas detailed in the project description of January 10, 1949 were not represented at the show: textiles, clothing, decoration, book design, newspaper design, graphic design, typography, photography, etc. […] We missed individually handcrafted products: furniture, textiles, ceramics, jewelry, sculpture, graphic art, stained glass, and many more besides.—The cult of

20 In 1925 Friedrich Kiesler's *City of Space* installation in Paris (Exposition internationale des arts décoratifs) had greatly impressed Bill with its freestanding frames.

21 For example, the photograph of an aluminum plate taken under a microscope was incorrectly referred to as the "stratification of a rock face" and the mushroom cloud generated by an atom bomb as the "water mushroom created during the explosion of an atom bomb in the ocean." See *NZZ*, n.d., May 1949 (ZHdK/MfGZ/DS/Konvolut SWB).

22 See the booklet accompanying the exhibition, which was compiled and designed by Bill, and the first plate (p. 39).

23 Scheidegger was centrally involved in producing the display panels and installing the exhibition. (Information from Jakob Bill, December 2012. See also the essay by Jakob Bill in this book, pp. 124–31.) Scheidegger remained Bill's closest colleague in the latter's Ulm years, too.

the industrial product seems in many cases outmoded. The knowledge of the beauty of technology is already over 20 years old. [...] Both in the exhibition and in the accompanying guide, Mr Max Bill may be accused of placing his name, his opinions, and his products in the foreground."[24]

Had Bill deceived the SWB and the Swiss authorities and created a show that consisted to a large extent of non-Swiss designs?[25] All the objects on display (furniture, lamps, instruments) came from Switzerland, and a good half of the 240 examples presented on the panels were likewise of Swiss provenance. The remainder came from the US (44), France (11), Italy (8), Finland (7), Sweden and Great Britain (both 6), Germany (4), Brazil (2), Denmark, the Netherlands, Japan, Russia, and Czechoslovakia (each 1). The show's critics started from the wrong assumption, however, namely that *Die gute Form* was to be a showcase of SWB talent. That was never Bill's intention. He did not want to present simply a compilation of "Werkbund objects" any more than he wished to mount a campaign to eradicate kitsch. Rather, he wanted to propose his own view of the world of objects and engage with the things that interested him. He thereby widened the traditional Werkbund concept of "truth to materials" in the direction of "truth to manufacture", which explains his focus upon new manufacturing methods. Bill's stance thereby contradicted the conventional wisdom at the SWB that truth to materials, correct construction, and fitness for purpose were sufficient requirements for beauty. Bill's approach to his theme proved much more dynamic than was the norm within the SWB and it may have been this that led his project in a different direction to the one originally intended. The process of writing his lecture "Beauty from function and as function" probably played a catalytic role in this respect.

The title "zweck + konstruktion = form" chosen by Bill for his initial exhibition concept, although pithy, was in truth avant-garde rhetoric from the prewar era and as such had long since lost its edge. Looked at critically, moreover, it contradicted the facts: designing does not proceed in the manner of a mathematical operation. The function of a utility object is not predetermined, but—like form, material, and construction—is a *sought* value. This must have dawned on Bill at the latest while he was working on the project (and was something he had earlier already practiced, for example in his design for a typewriter). When he gave the lecture "Beauty from function and as function" in autumn 1948, he had turned away from the bipolar thinking of the "hard" avant-garde ("function + construction = beauty") and in essence had returned to the classic Vitruvian Triad, in which beauty is *part of the task* and not the result.[26] This train of thought emerges in the following passage from the lecture:

24 Letter from the Basel branch of the SWB to Bill, June 8, 1949 (ZHdK/MfGZ/DS/Konvolut SWB).

25 The costs were modest even by the standards of their day: the entire budget for both sets of panels was CHF 35,000, of which the SWB paid CHF 15,000. Bill's fee amounted to CHF 8,000, including the production of the two sets of 80 panels (ZHdK/MfGZ/DS/Konvolut SWB).

26 For Vitruvius, *utilitas, firmitas,* and *venustas*—i.e. function, a solid structure, and beauty—were the three principles of a successful work of architecture.

"If we place particular value on something being beautiful, it's because pure functionality, in its narrow sense, is not what concerns us in the long term. We should no longer have to demand functionality—it ought to be a matter of course. But beauty is less self-evident, and ideas about what is beautiful or not beautiful often differ. That's why it's easier to keep on calling for functionality. The pursuit of beauty is much more difficult; it requires a greater effort, and succeeds only under particular creative conditions, when the idea of form meshes harmoniously with the particular task in hand. The two preconditions for this are first, the right commission, and second, the competence to design."[27]

In 1952, in the preface to his book *Form,* Bill noted that both his lecture of October 1948 and the exhibition half a year later had "stirred up controversy" inside and outside the Werkbund. He thanked his "esteemed master and friend" Henry van de Velde, SWB chairman Hans Finsler, architect Alfred Roth, and director of the Basel Kunstmuseum Georg Schmidt for their support and their "diplomatic skill at smoothing the waters."[28]

It is difficult for us today to see quite what was so provocative about Bill's vision. Is it possible that regional animosities within the SWB also played a role? (The fact that Bill featured too few works by members overall, and within those few, too many from Zurich and too few from Basel?) Or were people upset by the fact that he looked at the derided concept of fashion in a new light? (This is conceivable, but Le Corbusier had done the same thing in *L'Esprit Nouveau,* and Bill made it clear that, in referring to fashion, he did not mean what was "in fashion" but rather the rooting of a work in a specific epoch.) Or was it the fact that he effectively introduced an "aesthetic of commercial goods" into the rating of good design? There seem to have been several ways of offending against taboos within the Werkbund.

The most sensitive taboo was probably his mention of the "idea of form": the recognition that the designer does not arrive unaided at a formally compelling solution even when guided by reason, but must adopt an aesthetically active role. But didn't Mies van der Rohe write the sentence: "Form as a goal inevitably ends in formalism."? Mies bequeathed us few written statements and each one therefore seems precious. But Bill saw that this sentence was incorrect, namely that form only leads to formalism if taken as a *starting point.* For him, good design does not arise automatically out of the functional performance and technical quality of an object, but must be treated as a requirement in its own right. Bill recognized form (once again) as the legitimate goal of the design of things. It is impossible for us today to see that as a scandal.

27 Max Bill, as note 13. See also p. 143.

28 Max Bill, *Form. Eine Bilanz der Formentwicklung um die Mitte des XX. Jahrhunderts,* (Basel, 1952), p. 4.

If Bill's stance at that time remained somewhat unusual in Switzerland and northern Europe, it fully resonated with the attitude of the Italian designers, with their more flexible approach to form. On the occasion of the 1936 Triennale, Giuseppe Pagano wrote in the catalog *Tecnica dell'abitazione*—in an observation referring to modern furniture but equally applicable to other categories of object—that, both as a tool and an integral component of the home, it had to fulfill economic, practical, technical, and aesthetic demands.[29] And in 1954 Marcello Nizzoli, chief designer at Olivetti, described the work of the designer as a task of coming to an agreement with the engineers in order to marry the technical functioning of the object with the aesthetic form visualized by the designer: an exacting process involving a mutual modification of function and form, under the direction of the designer.[30] This was precisely Bill's attitude, too.

One detail is highly revealing in this context: Bill asked the Swiss master coachbuilder Hermann Graber in a letter to let him know when he found "a major improvement" in car design.[31] This shows that, for Bill, aesthetics is oriented towards "progress" in general and is not merely a subjective matter of personal likes and dislikes.

The question that now arises is this: is *Die gute Form* an example of dictatorship of taste? Was the project an attempt to launch a normative design ethic? This is primarily how posterity has viewed Bill's exhibition since 1968. But is it right?

Going through the panels of *Die gute Form,* we are struck by the wealth and heterogeneity of the examples. Bill is interested not in a deductive approach based on overall headings, but in the coherence of the individual object, which he looks at closely and summarizes in an economic language. He employs a wide spectrum of argument in his comments and reasoning. He does not classify the object within an existing conceptual matrix, but finds a few fitting words for each object. And since the genetic substance of these selected objects is in each case different, they assume correspondingly different forms. Take the panel with the Barcelona chair by Mies van der Rohe, the anonymous folding canvas chair, and Eero Saarinen's womb chair: they are all different, but each right in its own way (p. 87). Bill shows no preference for a particular type and dictates no stylistic direction. His commentaries are intended to encourage the public to develop their own eye for different qualities. His openness towards the diversity of solutions is an expression of his conviction that, for every design, new and different factors specific to the commission must be taken into account. This is an understanding of design as a process of intuitive reflection. We

29 "Il mobile moderno pensato e realizzato come un utensile e parte integrante dell'abitazione—esigenze economiche, pratiche, techniche, estetiche." Giuseppe Pagano, *Tecnica dell'abitazione* (Milan, 1937), p. 12.

30 Marcello Nizzoli, "Konsequentes Design" (first published in Italian in *Stile Industria,* 1954), in German in Hans Wichmann, *Italien. Design 1945 bis heute* (Munich, 1988), pp. 248–49.

31 m., b. + j. b. f.

might also use the Aristotelian term "entelechy", according to which a task already contains its own solution—albeit with the important reservation that, in Bill's view, the designer always retains a discretionary power for which he takes personal responsibility and should use in a convincing manner. Many episodes and constants in Bill's life probably have their origins here: his friendship with Henry van de Velde, the idea for *Die gute Form,* for his lecture "Beauty from function and as function", his book *Form,* and probably also his involvement in Ulm. (Years later Bill accused the designers at the Hochschule für Gestaltung of stylistic uniformity and insisted that no one could say the same about him.)[32] In his eyes, "good design" is the compelling form of a good object.

The success of the awards that were established (directly or indirectly) as a result of the exhibition would later attract criticism from Bill. In 1961 he spoke with irritation of what had come of out his initiative, of the great deal of "drivel, bluffing, hair-splitting and intellectual swindling," and in the same context poked fun at the term "industrial form" (*industrieform*) in Germany: "something has form or it hasn't. it doesn't have *industrial form.* what's that supposed to refer to—the form of the industry, its production methods, its organization or its products?" He thereby stressed that "*die gute form,* in line with its premise, wanted nothing to do with 'fancy design' [*gestalterei*]."[33] He considered that the shape or form of an object should be judged from the perspective of its practical use and he correspondingly saw "good design" as altogether a matter of how a product handled in practice. He sharply criticized the fact that many objects were winning prizes purely on the superficial criteria of their outward form, without being trialled in real life, and for this reason took himself off the award juries. Under "good design" he had imagined something that was both simpler and more comprehensive. Couching it within a framework of design philosophy had not been his main intention. (Even if he himself—like Wilhelm Braun-Feldweg and a number of others—provided a template for just such a framework, in particular with the introduction to his book *Form.*) Bill was now unpleasantly surprised by the misguided offspring that had issued from the project—and made efforts to contest his paternity.

Both in Bill's exhibition *Die gute Form* and in his book *Form* (in which he condenses and discusses in more detail the examples he has assembled), what is "good" about the design is always understood as an additional property of the object. From the way he writes, it is clear that "good design" is an attribute and can hence be explained and verified through argument and reasoning.

32 "Interview mit Max Bill", in Herbert Lindinger (ed.), *Hochschule für Gestaltung Ulm. Die Moral der Gegenstände* (Berlin, 1986), p. 66.

33 Max Bill, "über die güte der guten form," in *form. Internationale Revue* 15 (1961), p. 32.

It was here that the annual award of Die gute Form SWB in the years 1952 to 1969 proved problematic. The mark of quality was being awarded without further discussion of the chief criteria and with no verifiable appraisal of the object. In the case of the probably thousands of products that received the award, "good design" was no longer an attribute but a label, merely a commendation by an invisible authority. Upon his resignation in 1955, chairman Hans Finsler sarcastically lamented his impotence even within his position of power: "In spring I had to place my signature beneath 250 'good design' awards even though I had never even seen the good designs." And he posed the key question that the Werkbund needed to ask itself: in eulogizing the design, did one not lose the feel for the whole? "What sort of importance do the *things* to whose design and quality the Werkbund is pledged have for people? What are the bases on which the Werkbund evaluates these things? What is the Werkbund's contribution to the creation of these things?"[34] In raising such issues, an awareness of a problem that many Werkbund members were failing to see, is manifested: namely, that the value of an object cannot being reduced to its design. This is precisely what does *not* happen in Bill's selection and in his commentaries, because Bill takes a reasoned approach to each object and does not treat formal quality as an absolute value split off from other criteria.

When, after more than fifteen years, the award Die gute Form SWB came to the "end of the line," explanations were found. In a clever commentary on the SWB's "tirelessly design-seeking eye," Antonio Hernandez wrote: "We shall not expect, however, that by adding together all the things, the sum total of our environment can be obtained." And he relativized the relevance of good design with the following argument: "It is not all the same, after all, whether I use a table lamp or a circulation pump—nothing against circulation pumps, but you and I have less to do with them than with a table lamp that stands before us every evening."[35]

Bill would not have accepted this pragmatic line of reasoning, however. For him, good design as the compelling form of a good product was always the epiphany of a better world—even in the darkness of a boiler room.

Doubts about the relevance of formal design grew ever stronger during the boom years, and the belief that design could make the world a better place ever weaker. The designer Victor Papanek argued for a broader concept of design and included "soft" factors such as personal associations and sociocultural conditions in his "function complex."[36] And in 1970 his contemporary, the sociologist and art historian Lucius Burckhardt, a generation younger than Finsler, half a generation younger than Bill,

34 Hans Finsler, "Der Werkbund und die Dinge," in: *SWB-Tagungsbericht* (St. Gallen, 1955), p. 28.

35 Antonio Hernandez: "Nach 15 Jahren: Bilanz der *Guten Form*", in *SWB-Kommentare,* supplement to the journal *Werk* 11 (1967), n. p.

36 Cf. Victor Papanek, *Design for the Real World. Human Ecology and Social Change,* (1st ed., 1971), Ch. 1: "What is Design? A Definition of the Function Complex" (Chicago, 1984), pp. 3–27.

and for many years—as a Swiss—the chairman of the German Werkbund, formulated this recognition of the limits of formal design in a significant statement: "The belief that a human environment can be produced through design is one of the most fundamental errors of the pioneers of the modern movement. People's environments are only visible and subject to formal design to a small extent. To a far greater extent, however, they consist of organizational and institutional factors. Changing this is a political task."[37]

For Burckhardt, this meant a more comprehensive concept of design: in his view, design also extended to the non-visible premises of the human environment, from the organization of time, tariff structures and communal living to laws and regulations. "Design is invisible" was Burckhardt's catchy term for this hidden dimension. The question is simply whether this viewpoint truly refutes Max Bill. For where Bill saw the limits of design, he, too, respected them and consequently made the move into politics precisely in order—he hoped—to change the marginal conditions.[38] Even if this endeavor proved largely unsuccessful and brought him little personal encouragement, it is clear from the panels documented here from the exhibition *Die gute Form* that Bill, too, was not trying to establish an aesthetic canon and that for him, too, design meant "design, not just shape!" (Burckhardt).

[37] Lucius Burckhardt, "Design heisst Entwurf, nicht Gestalt!," in *design? Internationales Design Zentrum (IDZ) Berlin,* vol. 1 (1970), n. p.

[38] Max Bill served on the City of Zurich parliament from 1961 to 1968 and as a parliamentarian (*Nationalrat*) in Bern from 1967 to 1971, in both cases as a member of the Swiss political party "Landesring der Unabhängigen" (Ring of Independents).

Claude Lichtenstein was born in Zurich in 1949. He studied architecture at the Swiss Federal Institute of Technology. From 1985 to 2001 he was curator of architecture and design at the Museum für Gestaltung, Zurich. Today Claude Lichtenstein teaches cultural history and design studies at a number of Swiss universities. He lives in Zurich. Major exhibitions with publications: *Unbekannt – vertraut. Anonymes Design im Schweizer Gebrauchsgerät seit 1920* (1987); *Brückenschläge: Robert Maillart* (1990); *Ferdinand Kramer. Architektur – Design – Einrichtung. Der Charme des Systematischen* (1991); *Stromlinienform* (1992); *Bruno Munari: Die Luft sichtbar machen* (1995); *R. Buckminster Fuller: Your PrivateSky – The Art of Design Science,* (1999), and vol. 2: *R. Buckminster Fuller: Your Private Sky – Diskurs* (2001); *As Found: The Discovery of The Ordinary* (2001); *Playfully Rigid: Swiss Architecture, Graphic Design, Product Design, 1950–2006* (2006).

Entrance to the Basel exhibition, with Max Bill's sculpture *rhythm in space*.

The entrance area with section 1: "Forms in nature, science, art and technology."

> Exhibition installation in the section 3: "Forms in home fittings and furnishings," with furniture display including folded and dismantled items (Colonial chair by Wilhelm Kienzle, Plio folding stool by Jacob Müller, and folding side table (designer unknown)).

Max Bill at the opening of the exhibition in May 1949, personally handing out copies of the booklet "Die gute Form: Sonderschau an der Schweizer Mustermesse" to arriving visitors. The illustrated guide was written by Bill to accompany the exhibition.

The display panels from the exhibition *Die gute Form* are today
housed in the Museum für Gestaltung Zürich/Design Collection.

Die gute Form

veranstaltet vom
Schweizerischen Werkbund (SWB)
mit Unterstützung des
Eidgenössischen Departement des Innern
und der Schweizer Mustermesse
nach Idee und Plan von
Architekt Max Bill Zürich

Unter einer guten Form
verstehen wir eine natürliche,
aus ihren funktionellen
und technischen Voraussetzungen
entwickelte Form eines Produktes,
das seinem Zweck ganz entspricht
und das gleichzeitig schön ist.
Nach diesen Gesichtspunkten
sind die Beispiele ausgewählt,
die wir hier zeigen.

Good Design

hosted by the
Schweizerischer Werkbund (SWB—Swiss
Federation of Architects, Artists, and Builders)
with the support of the
Federal Department of the Interior
and the Swiss Samples Fair, and
based on the ideas and plans of
architect Max Bill, Zurich

We understand "good design" to mean a natural
form for a product developed out of its functional
and technical requirements and which fulfills
the intended purpose in a visually appealing way.
The examples shown here were selected
according to these criteria.

Hochformen der Materie

Steinsalz-Kristalle
in wasserklarer Würfelform
Fundort Wiediczka (Galizien)

Kieselerde
Sinterbildung, Quellabsatz
schichtförmige Lagerung der Materie
Fundort Böhmen

Schwefelkies (3 x natürliche Grösse)
Gruppierung von Oktaedern
zu einem grossen Oktaeder
Fundort Brosso (Piemont)

Matter in Its Highest Form

Rock-salt crystal
in limpid cubic form
Found in Wiediczka (Galicia)

Silica
Sinter formation, source deposit
Sedimentary material layers
Found in Bohemia

Pyrite (3 × natural size)
Grouping of several octahedrons
into one large octahedron
Found in Brosso (Piedmont)

Forms in nature, science, art and technology

Strömungsformen

Chemischer Rauch
Harmonische Formen
natürliches Bewegungsspiel
aufsteigenden Rauches

Rauchpilz
entstanden durch Abwurf einer Atombombe
zentrale Ausdehnung von einem Punkt aus
bis 18000 Meter Höhe

Anilinfarbe im Wasser
Schlierenbildung sinkender Partikel
harmonische Linienformung

Flow Forms

Chemical smoke
Harmonious forms
Natural play of movement
of rising smoke

Mushroom cloud generated by explosion
of an atom bomb
Central expansion from a single point
up to a height of 18,000 m

Aniline dye in water
Streaks formed by sinking particles
Harmonious linear formation

Bewegungen

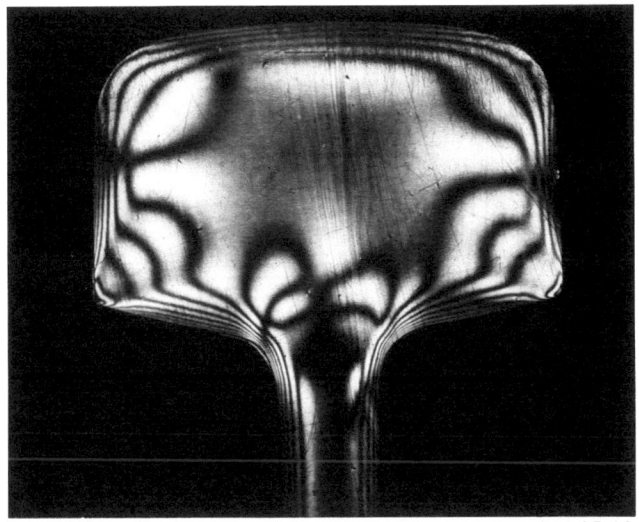

Spannungsfelder
sichtbar gemacht im polarisierten Licht
Untersuchung an Celluloidprofil

Bischof, Zürich

Ueberschneidung (Interferenz)
zweier Wellengruppen
die durch zwei Bewegungspole
auf einer Quecksilberoberfläche entstehen

Bischof, Zürich

Edgerton, New York

Bewegung eines Golfspielers
aufgenommen mit dem Stroboscop
von H. E. Edgerton

Movements

Tension fields
made visible in polarizing light
Investigation of celluloid profile

Intersection (interference)
between two groups of waves
generated by two movement poles
on a mercury surface

Movement of a golfer
recorded with the stroboscope
of H. E. Edgerton

Forms in nature, science, art and technology

Die Grenze des Sichtbaren

Struktur der Oberfläche
einer angeätzten Aluminiumplatte
Vergrösserung 53'000 fach
aufgenommen mit dem Elektronen-Mikroskop
Trüb, Täuber & Co. AG. Zürich

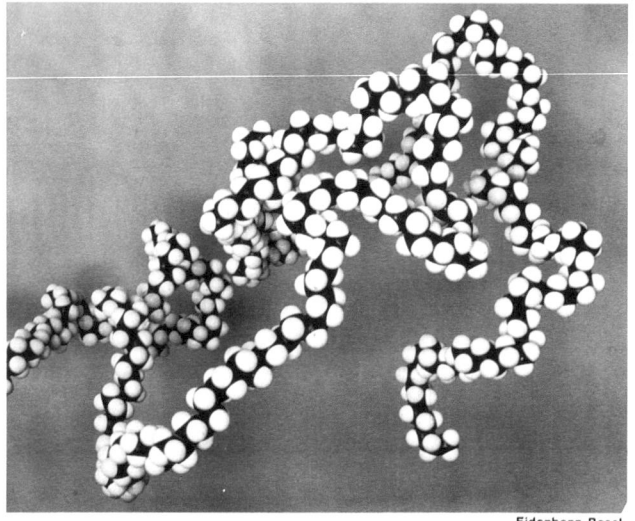

Molekül-Modell von Hydrokautschuk
Grundstruktur der Materie
wissenschaftlich dargestellt
Kohlenstoffkette (schwarz)
zugeordnete Wasserstoffatome (weiss)
Vergrösserung ca. 130 millionenfach
Foto Eidenbenz für
Physikalisch-Chemische Anstalt
der Universität Basel

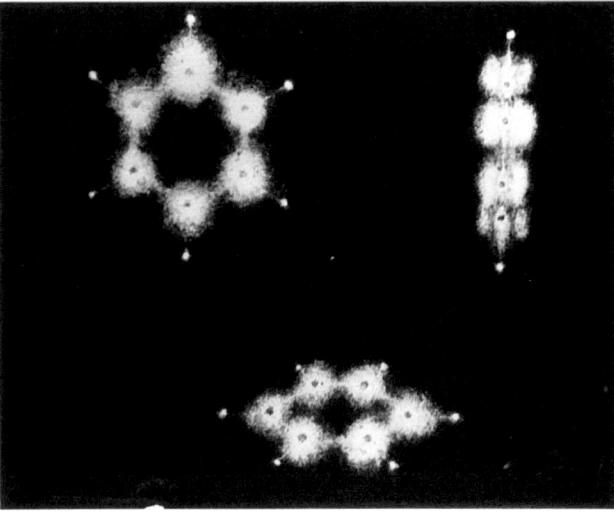

Benzolring in drei verschiedenen Positionen
225 millionenfache Vergrösserung
je 6 Kohlenstoffatome und 6 Wasserstoffatome
bilden ein Benzolmolekül
Darstellung von H. Haffenrichter, Heidelberg

The Limits of the Visible

Surface texture of an etched
aluminum plate
53,000 × magnification
Recorded with an electron microscope
Trüb, Täuber & Co. AG, Zurich

Molecular model of hydrogenated rubber
Basic structure of matter
depicted scientifically
Carbon chain (black)
with linked hydrogen atoms (white)
Approx. 130 million × magnification
Photo from Eidenbenz for the
Institute of Physics and Chemistry
at the University of Basel

Benzene ring in three different positions
225 million × magnification
A benzene molecule has six carbon and
six hydrogen atoms
Depiction by H. Haffenrichter, Heidelberg

Mathematik räumlich dargestellt

Realteil einer mathematischen Funktion
In der Mathematik können Formeln
zu harmonischen Gebilden werden
und dadurch empfindungsmässig jedermann
zugänglich sein

Oberfläche von Carl Pearson
plastische Darstellung eines Theorems
unbestreitbarer ästhetischer Reiz der
Darstellung einer mathematischen Wahrheit

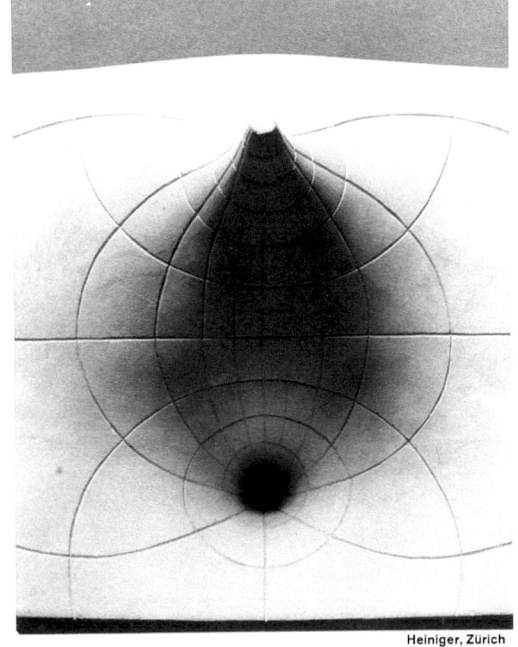

Plastische Teildarstellung
der elliptischen Funktion $W = p'(U)$
sinnlich wahrnehmbare Schönheit
eines mathematischen Gedankens

Spatial Representation of Mathematics

Real part of a mathematical function
In mathematics, formulas can be depicted
as harmonious structures
and thus rendered perceptible to everyone

Surface by Carl Pearson
Plastic representation of a theory
Undeniable aesthetic appeal of the
depiction of a mathematical reality

Plastic partial representation
of the elliptic function $W = p'(U)$
Sensually perceptible beauty
of a mathematical concept

Forms in nature, science, art and technology

Plastische Kunst

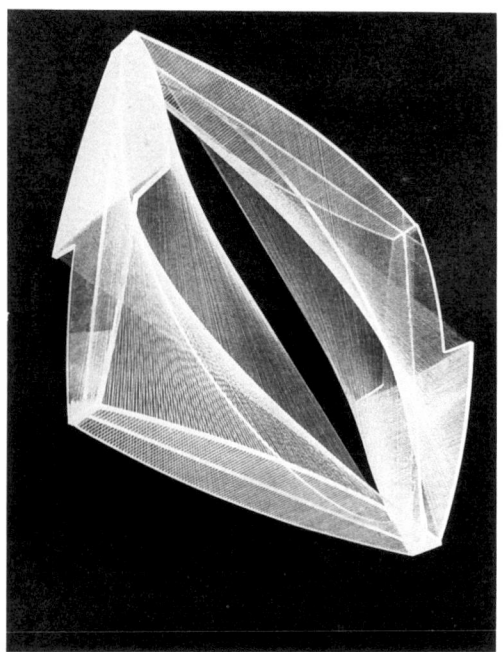

Präzis geordnete Linienbündel
ergeben ein durchsichtiges,
begrenztes Volumen
Ausführung in Plexiglas
Plastik ‚Lineare Konstruktion' 1942-43
von Naum Gabo, Connecticut

Museum of Modern Art, New York

Band mit paralleler Begrenzung
konkave und konvexe Raumformen
ohne Begrenzung
Plastik ‚Kontinuität' 1947
von Max Bill, Zürich

Herdeg, Zürich

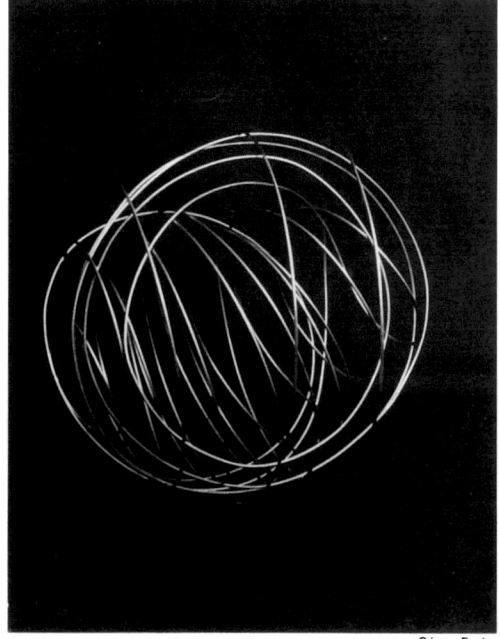

Ein einziges Material in gleichbleibender Stärke
als Träger eines dynamischen Ausdrucks
ein unbegrenzter Raum,
der durch Linien gebildet wird
Plastik ‚Revolution' 1946
von Georges Vantongerloo, Paris

César, Paris

Sculptural Art

Precisely arranged bundles of lines
generate a transparent,
delimited volume
Executed in Plexiglas
Naum Gabo, Connecticut,
Linear Construction, 1942–43

Band with parallel edges
Concave and convex spatial forms
without delimitation
Max Bill, Zurich, *Continuity,* 1947

A single material of uniform thickness
as bearer of dynamic expression
An unlimited space formed by lines
Georges Vantongerloo, Paris,
Revolution, 1946

Plastische Kunst

Verschiedene Formen und Rhytmen
verschiedene Materialien
Gestaltung charakteristischer Ausdrücke
aus dem Bildhaueratelier
von Constatin Brancousi, Paris

Scheinbar amorphe Form
nach künstlerischen Gesichtspunkten
gestaltet
Gesetzmässigkeit der Zufallserscheinung
Plastik ‚Alon' 1942
von Hans Arp, Meudon-Paris

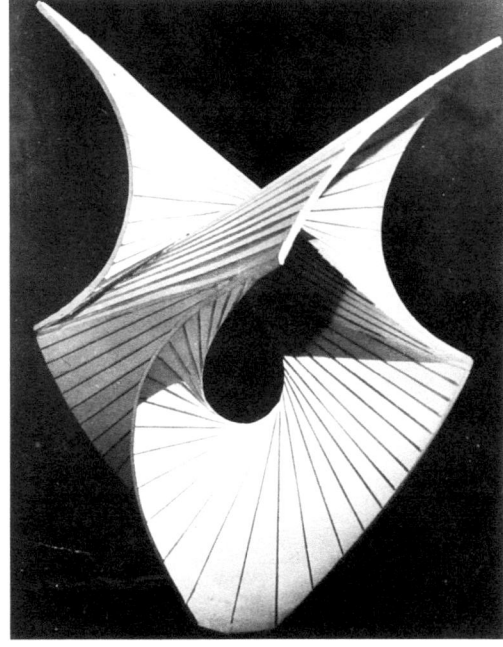

Plastik ‚Konstruktion' 1939
von Anton Pevsner, Paris
Fläche aus geraden Linien gebildet
überraschende Raumwirkung
konstruktive Gestaltung
als Ausdruck von Harmonie

Sculptural Art

Various forms and rhythms
Various materials
Formation of characteristic expressions
from the sculpture studio of
Constantin Brancusi, Paris

Seemingly amorphous form
designed according to artistic criteria
Random appearance actually obeys certain laws
Hans Arp, Meudon-Paris, *Alon,* 1942

Antoine Pevsner, Paris, *Construction,* 1939
Surface formed from straight lines
Surprising effect in space
Constructive design as expression of harmony

Forms in nature, science, art and technology

Formen der Technik

Schiffs-Verstellpropeller
ermöglicht ohne Umstellen der Maschine
Vorwärtsfahrt, Halt und Rückwärtsfahrt
vollkommene Form
aus wohlüberlegter Funktion
Hersteller Escher-Wyss
Maschinenfabriken AG., Zürich

Heiniger, Zürich

Versuchsanlage
der Firma Brown Boveri & Co. AG.
zur Beobachtung der Wettereinwirkung
auf Isolatoren und Höchstspannungsapparate

Fräsblatt für Nuten
reinste Zweckmässigkeit der Formen
verschiedene Materialien je nach der Funktion
Hersteller Albert Lenartz, Bühlach

Heiniger, Zürich

Technological Forms

Variable-pitch ship's propeller
enables forward, stop, and reverse movement
without adjusting the machine
Perfect form derived from well-considered function
Manufacturer: Escher-Wyss Maschinenfabriken
AG, Zurich

Testing facility
of the company Brown Boveri & Co. AG
for observing the effects of weather
on isolators and ultra-high-voltage apparatuses

Milling blade for grooves
Purest functionality of forms
Various materials according to function
Manufacturer: Albert Lenartz, Bühlach

Maschinenformen

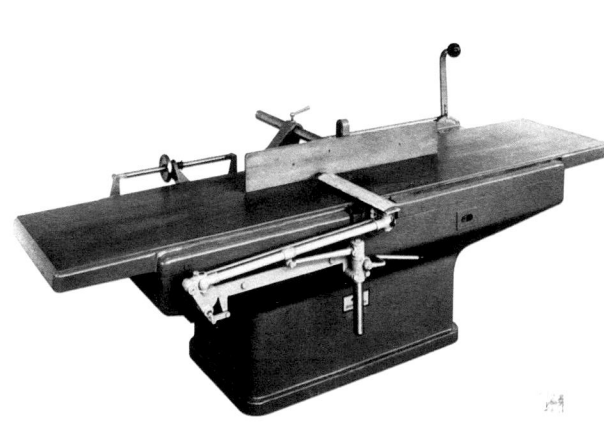

Abrichtmaschine
für Holzbearbeitung
klare, zweckmässige Gestaltung
Hersteller Georg Fischer AG. Schaffhausen

Präzisions-Fräsmaschine
für rationellste Arbeitsweise
Tisch fest montiert
in Längs-, Quer- und Vertikalrichtung
verschiebbar
Hersteller Schäublin S.A. Bévilard

Schleif- und Poliermaschine
mit elektrischem Antrieb
übersichtliche Gesamtanordnung
harmonische Durchbildung,
einschliesslich Firmenmarke
Herst. Aug. Joos, Maschinenfabrik, Frauenfeld

Machine Forms

Planing machine
for woodworking
Clear, functional design
Manufacturer: Georg Fischer AG, Schaffhausen

Precision milling machine
for the most rational working method
Permanently mounted table can be shifted
in longitudinal, horizontal, and vertical directions
Manufacturer: Schäublin S.A. Bévillard

Grinding and polishing machine
with electric drive
Clear overall arrangement
Harmonious design,
including company logo
Manufacturer: Aug. Joos machine factory, Frauenfeld

Forms in nature, science, art and technology

Elektrotechnik

3 Einphasentransformatoren
als 42000 kVA Transformatorengruppe
Unterwerk Bickingen der Bern. Kraftwerke
Dimensionen entwickelt mit Rücksicht auf
einfachen Bahntransport
Hersteller Brown Boveri & Co. AG. Baden

Überschlag an einer 18-gliedrigen Hängekette
Unterschlagspannung 1100 kV
im Hochspannungslaboratorium
der Firma Brown Boveri & Co. AG.

Kommandoraum
Wasserkraftwerk La Dernier der Cie. Vaudoise
des forces motrices des lacs de Joux et de
l'Orbe, Lausanne
Pult mit allen Apparaten und Instrumenten für
die Generatoren, Transformatoren u. Schalter
Hersteller Brown Boveri & Co. AG. Baden

Electrical Engineering

Three single-phase transformers
as 42,000 kVA transformer group
Bickingen substation, Bern power plants
Dimensions developed for simple rail transport
Manufacturer: Brown Boveri & Co. AG, Baden

Flashover on an 18-link hanging chain
Low voltage of 1,100 kV
in high-voltage laboratory
of the company Brown Boveri & Co. AG

Control center
of the hydroelectric power plant La Dernier
run by the company Vaudoise
des forces motrices des lacs de Joux et de
l'Orbe, Lausanne
Desk with all apparatuses and instruments for the
generators, transformers, and switches
Manufacturer: Brown Boveri & Co. AG, Baden

Messgeräte

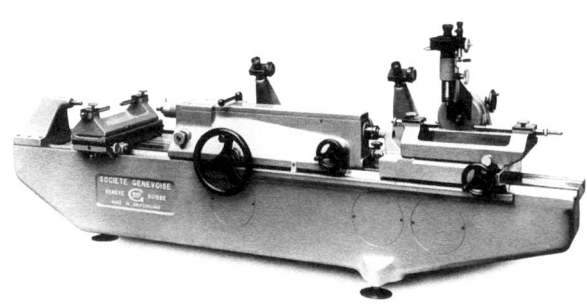

Genauigkeits-Messmaschine
Ablesbarkeit bis 1/1000 mm
sorgfältige formale Durchbildung aller Teile
harmonische Gesamtwirkung
Hersteller Société Genevoise
d'Instruments de Physik, Genève

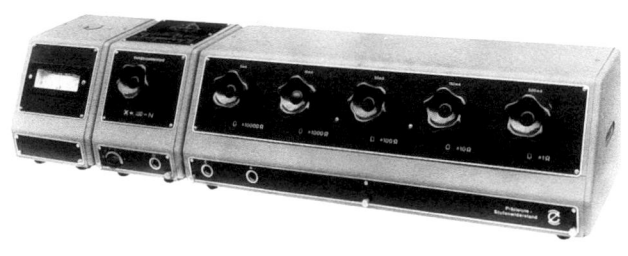

Präzisions-Messbrücke
aus Präzisions-Stufenwiderstand,
Verhältniswiderstand und Null-Indikator
zur Messung des Widerstands-Wertes
elektrischer Präzisions-Widerstände
Harmonische Durchbildung aller Bestandteile
übersichtliche Beschriftungen
Hersteller Contraves AG. Zürich

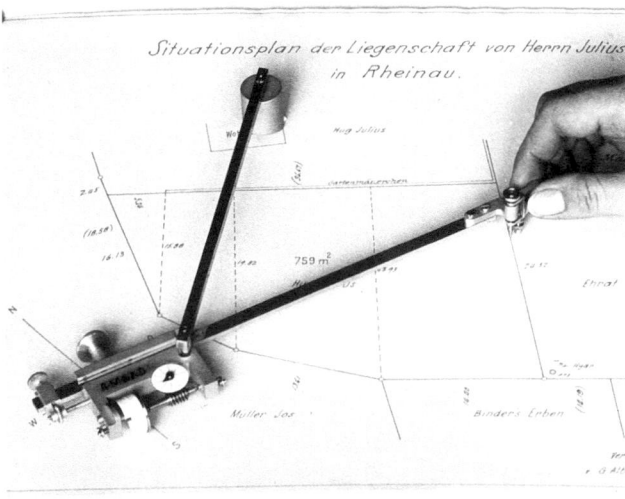

Planimeter
Instrument zur Ausmessung der Flächen
konstruktive Durchbildung
auf Grund der reinen Funktion
fast unveränderte Form seit 80 Jahren
Hersteller A. J. Amsler & Co. Schaffhausen

Measuring Devices

Precision measuring machine
Readable up to 1/1000 mm
Carefully considered formal design of all parts
Harmonious overall look
Manufacturer: Société Genevoise d'Instruments de Physik, Geneva

Precision measuring bridge
made up of precision step-by-step resistor,
ratio resistor, and zero indicator
for measuring the resistance value of
electric precision resistances
Harmonious design of all components
Clearly labeled
Manufacturer: Contraves AG, Zurich

Planimeter
Instrument for measuring area
Structural design based on pure function
Form nearly unchanged for eighty years
Manufacturer: A.J. Amsler & Co., Schaffhausen

Forms in nature, science, art and technology

Waagen

Zählwaage
klare Gestaltung der Details
zweckmässige Formgebung der Schalen
Hersteller Max Keller Waagenfabrik, Zürich

Feinwaage
harmonisch elegante Formgebung
alle feinen Teile eingeschlossen
Entwurf Allen-Bowden Ltd. Leamington (GB)
Hersteller W.& T. Avery Ltd. Birmingham

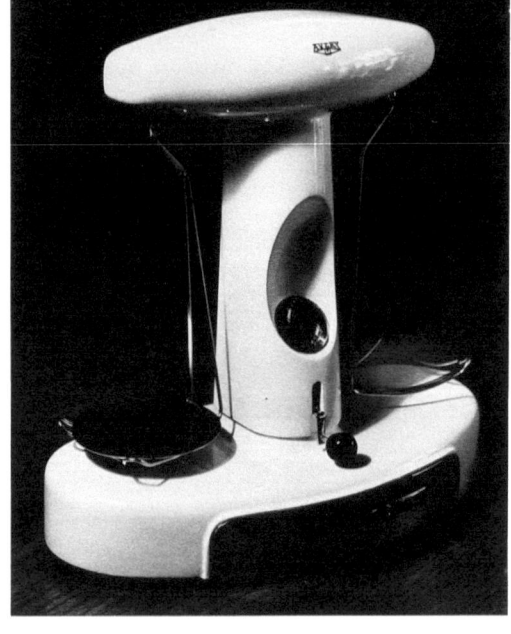

Feinwaage
asymmetrische innere Konstruktion
bestimmt die Aussenform
Hersteller Max Keller Waagenfabrik, Zürich

Scales

Counting scale
Clear design of details
Functional tray form
Manufacturer: Max Keller Waagenfabrik, Zurich

Fine scale
Harmonious, elegant design
All fine parts enclosed
Design: Allen-Bowdon Ltd., Leamington (UK)
Manufacturer: W. & T. Avery Ltd., Birmingham

Fine scale
Asymmetrical inner workings
determine outer form
Manufacturer: Max Keller Waagenfabrik, Zurich

Vergrösserungs-Instrumente

Lupe
Optik in Metall gefasst
einfachste traditionelle Formgebung
Hersteller Wild, Heerbrugg

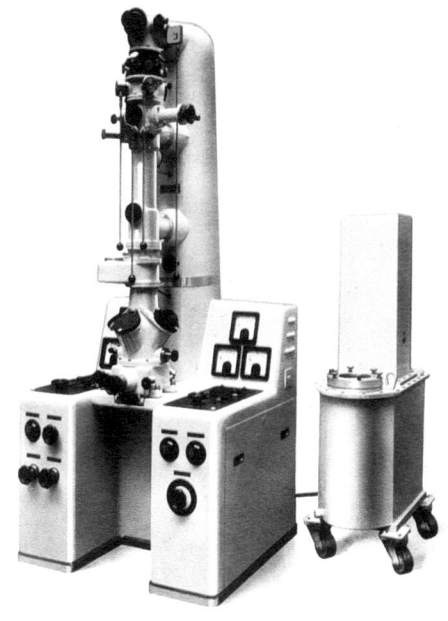

Elektronen-Mikroskop
direkte Vergrösserung bis 12'000fach
Form aus der Funktion entwickelt
harmonische Gesamtwirkung
Hersteller Trüb, Täuber & Co. Zürich

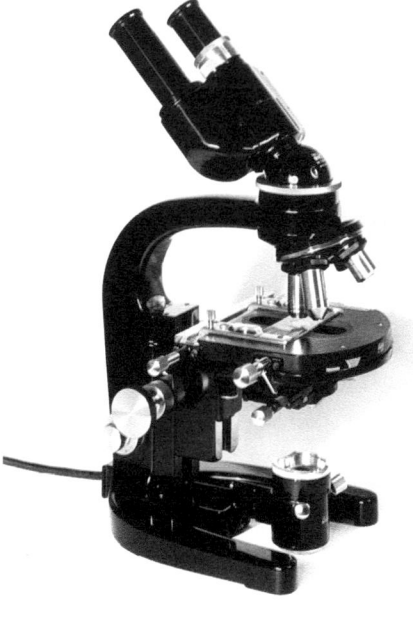

Forschungsmikroskop
für Beobachtung mit zwei Augen
sorgfältige formale Gestaltung
einheitliche Schraubendurchbildung
Hersteller AG. Heinrich Wild's Erben
Geodätische Instrumente, Heerbrugg

Magnifying Instruments

Magnifying glass
Lens set in metal frame
Simple, traditional design
Manufacturer: Wild, Heerbrugg

Electron microscope
Direct magnification up to 12,000 ×
Form developed out of function
Harmonious overall look
Manufacturer: Trüb, Täuber & Co., Zurich

Scientific microscope
for stereo observation
Carefully considered formal design
Uniform screw design
Manufacturer: AG Heinrich Wild's Erben
Geodätische Instrumente, Heerbrugg

Forms in nature, science, art and technology

Werkzeuge des Technikers

Präzisionszeichenmaschine
Parallelführung vermittels Stahlbändern
Zeichenkopf um 360° drehbar
äusserste Präzision in Funktion und Gestaltung
Hersteller O-Key AG. Zürich
Vertrieb Ozalid AG. Zürich

Nivellier-Instrument
kleinste Dimensionen, geringes Gewicht
mit neuem Gelenkkopf-Stativ
Präzisionsarbeit auch in der Formgebung
Hersteller Kern & Co. AG. Aarau

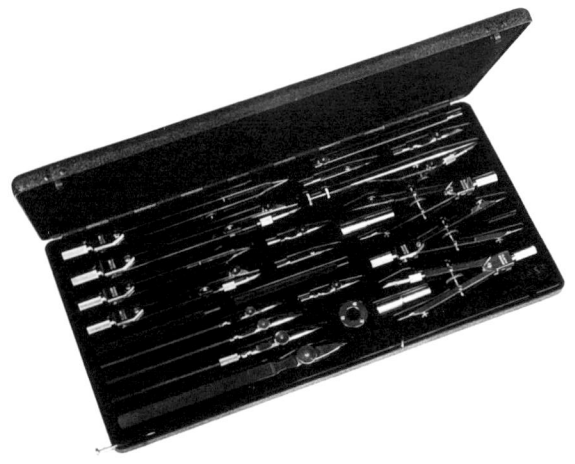

Reisszeug
sorgfältige Durchbildung der Instrumente
Kasten mit Bakelit-Einsatz
leicht zu reinigen und staubfrei zu halten
Hersteller AG. Heinrich Wild's Geodätische
Instrumente, Heerbrugg

Technicians' Tools

Precision drafting machine
Parallel guidance using steel bands
Drawing head can be rotated 360°
Extreme precision in function and design
Manufacturer: O-Key AG, Zurich
Sold by: Ozalid AG, Zurich

Leveling instrument
Smallest dimensions, low weight
with new hinged-head tripod
Precision work in design as well
Manufacturer: Kern & Co. AG, Aarau

Set of drawing instruments
Carefully considered design of instruments
Case with Bakelite insert
Easy to clean and keep dust-free
Manufacturer: AG Heinrich Wild's
Geodätische Instrumente, Heerbrugg

Hand-Griffe

Koffergriffe
nach der Hand geformt
dass Gewichte nicht zu sehr anstrengen
Ausführung in Kunstharz
Entwurf Thomas Lamb, New York

Schraubenzieher
Versuch einer Formgebung
unter Berücksichtigung der Handform
Studie aus dem Institute of Design, Chicago

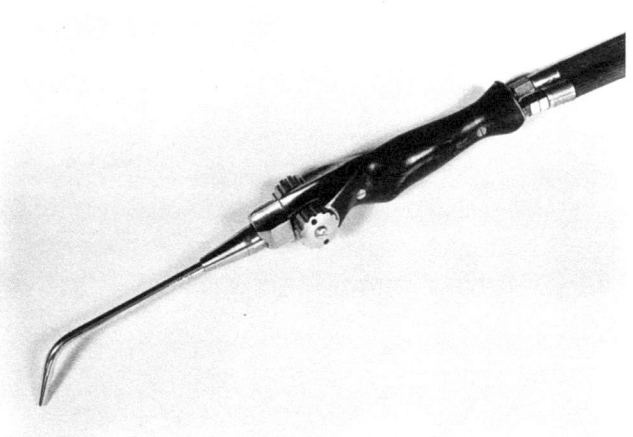

Lötapparat
mit Glasgebläse
sinnvolle Gestaltung mit handgerechtem Griff
Entwurf Thomas Lamb, New York

Handles

Suitcase handles
shaped to fit the hand
so that carrying weight is less tiring
Executed in synthetic resin
Design: Thomas Lamb, New York

Screwdriver
Attempt at finding a shape
to fit the hand
Study from the Institute of Design, Chicago

Soldering device
with glass blower
Sensible design with easy-grip handle
Design: Thomas Lamb, New York

Landes- und Regionalplanung

Bepflanzungsplan für Südrussland
zur Veränderung d. klimatischen Verhältnisse
gegen Dürre und Versteppung
grosse, durchgehende Baumbänder
Kleinteilung durch generelle Baumstreifen

Dokument Pravda

Das Tennessee-Flusstal
Regierungsprojekt der Tennessee-Valley
Authority
zur Behebung der Ueberschwemmungsgefahr
zur Nutzbarmachung der Wasserkräfte
und Schiffbarmachung des Flusses

Schutzgebiet Greifensee (Kanton Zürich)
als Erholungsgelände der Stadt Zürich
weitgehende Bauverbote z. Schutz d. Seeufer
als regierungsrätliche Verordnung in Kraft

National and Regional Planning

Planting plan for south Russia
to change climate conditions,
combatting drought and desertification
Large, continuous bands of trees
Small divisions through general tree strips

The Tennessee River Valley
Tennessee Valley Authority government project
for eliminating the danger of floods
while harnessing water power
and making river navigable

Greifensee nature reserve (Canton Zurich)
as recreational landscape for the City of Zurich
An extensive construction ban to protect
the lakeshore is enforced as a directive of the
government council

Forms in planning and architecture

Stadtplanungen

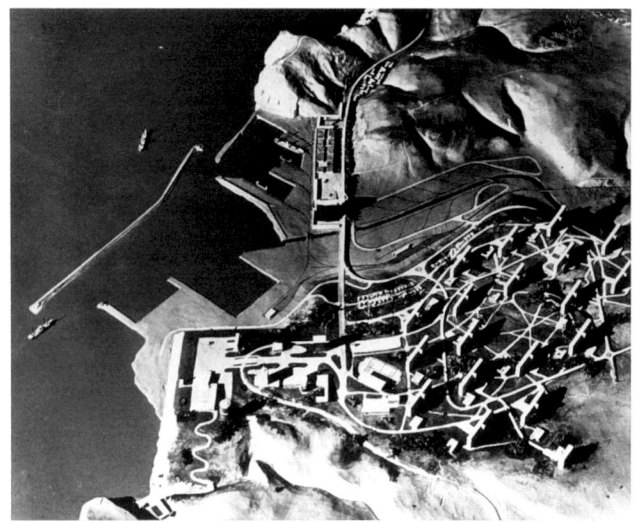

Vorschlag für die Bebauung
der Hafenstadt Nemours (Nordafrika)
Orientierung der Wohnblöcke
gegen die Nordseite (Meer)
Projekt Architekten Le Corbusier und
Pierre Jeanneret, Paris

Quartier ‚Slotermeer'
aus dem Erweiterungsplan von Amsterdam
Mischbebauung
aus hohen und niedrigen Gebäuden
Ausnutzung der Lage am Meer
genehmigtes Projekt von 1939
Entwurf Amt für öffentliche Arbeiten

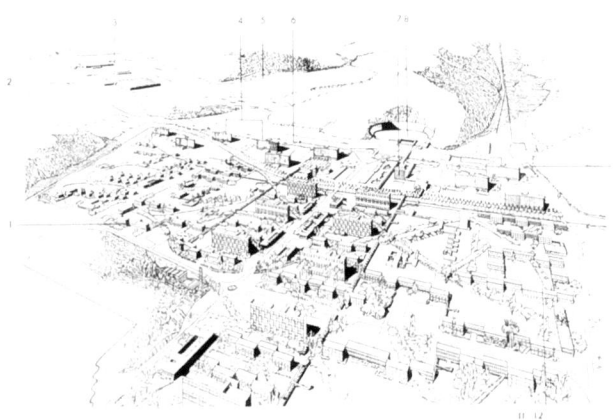

Motorenstadt, Brasilien
Stadtneugründung mit Industrie (3)
hohe und niedrige Bebauung gemischt
keine Kreuzung von Geh- und Fahrwegen
Projekt Architekten Wiener & Sert, New York

City Planning

Proposal for development
of the harbor city of Nemours (North Africa)
Orientation of housing blocks
away from the north side (sea)
Project by architects Le Corbusier and
Pierre Jeanneret, Paris

"Slotermeer" quarter
from the expansion plan for Amsterdam
Mixed development
of high and low buildings
Taking advantage of site on the sea
Approved project from 1939
Design: Office of Public Works

Motor City, Brazil
Newly founded city with industry (3)
High and low buildings mixed
No intersection of roadways and walkways
Project by architects Wiener & Sert, New York

Neusiedlungen

Juba-City
Dorf der Farm-Arbeiter-Genossenschaft
mit ca. 100 festen Wohnhäusern
und ca. 300 transportablen Häusern
für Wanderarbeiter
Architekten Cairns & DeMars

Genossenschaftsdorf Greenbelt (USA)
885 Wohneinheiten, ca. 3000 Einwohner
Anlage der Wohnhäuser um einen Kern
mit Gemeinschaftsbauten
Architekten Hale Walker, Ellington & Wadsworth

Channel Heights
kleine Ortschaft für ca. 2500 Personen
in 600 Wohneinheiten verschiedener Typen
Einfache solide konstruktive Durchführung
Architekt Richard J. Neutra, Los Angeles

Planned Towns

Juba City
Village of the Farm Worker's Association
with approx. 100 permanent residences
and approx. 300 mobile homes
for migrant workers

Greenbelt (USA) cooperative village
885 residential units, approx. 3,000 inhabitants
Homes laid out around a core
with community buildings
Architects: Hale Walker, Ellington & Wadsworth

Channel Heights
Small town for approx. 2,500 persons
in 600 residential units of various types
Simple, solid construction
Architect: Richard J. Neutra, Los Angeles

Differenzierte Wohnquartiere

Werkbundsiedlung Neubühl, Zürich
195 Wohneinheiten verschiedener Typen
Einzelzimmer-Wohnung bis Fünfzimmer-Haus
so angelegt, dass für alle freie Seesicht
Architekten Haefeli, Hubacher, Steiger, Moser,
Roth, Artaria, Schmidt

Bebauungsvorschlag für Prilly-Lausanne
verschiedene Haustypen unter
Ausnützung des hügeligen Geländes
nach räumlichen Gesichtspunkten geplant
Architekten Haefeli, Mo ser, Steiger
und Dr. M. Hottinger

Wolgensinger, Zürich

Siedlung Drancy bei Paris
gemischte Bebauungsform
Wohntürme für Kleinfamilien
Konstruktion: Stahlskelett mit
vorfabrizierten Aussenwandelementen
Architekten Beaudouin & Lods, Paris

Differentiated Residential Neighborhoods

Neubühl Werkbund Development, Zurich
195 residential units of various types,
from studios to five-room apartments,
designed to afford everyone an unobstructed
lake view
Architects: Haefeli, Hubacher, Steiger, Moser,
Roth, Artaria, Schmidt

Development proposal for Prilly-Lausanne
Various housing types taking advantage
of the hilly site
Planned according to spatial aspects
Architects: Haefeli, Moser, Steiger
and Dr. M. Hottinger

Drancy development, near Paris
Mixed development form
Tower blocks for small families
Structure: steel skeleton with
prefabricated exterior wall elements
Architects: Beaudouin & Lods, Paris

Wohnhaus-Gruppen

Häusergruppe am Hügel
abgetreppte Gärten, Ausnutzung d. Geländes
dichte Baugruppe ohne Beeinträchtigung
der Bewohner
Architekt Richard J. Neutra, Los Angeles

Mehrfamilienhäuser in Zürich
Schrägstellung, daher überall freie Sicht
grosse Wohnterrassen vor den Wohnraumen
saubere konstruktive Gestaltung
Architekten Alfred & Emil Roth, Zürich
Mitarbeiter Marcel Breuer

Finsler, Zürich

Reihen-Einfamilienhäuser
für Ingenieure der Fabrik Sunila (Finnland)
Verschiebung der Bauten in der Front
daher grösstmögliche Trennung
Architekten Aino & Alvar Aalto, Helsinki

Housing Ensembles

Housing complex on a hill
Terraced gardens making use of the entire grounds
Dense ensemble without negative
effects for residents
Architect: Richard J. Neutra, Los Angeles

Multifamily houses in Zurich
Staggered layout ensures views from all apartments
Large terraces set before the living rooms
Clean-lined structural design
Architects: Alfred & Emil Roth, Zurich
Associate: Marcel Breuer

Single-family row houses
for engineers in the Sunila factory (Finland)
The fronts of buildings are shifted for the
greatest possible separation of the units
Architects: Aino & Alvar Aalto, Helsinki

Forms in planning and architecture

Bürohäuser

Bürogebäude als Gruppe geplant
Mischung von niedrigen und hohen Bauten
intensive Bodennutzung, trotzdem weiträumig
Baukomplex Rockefeller Center, New-York
Architekten Reinhard & Hofmeister, Corbett
Harriman & Mac Murray, Hood & Fouilhoux

Gesundheits- und Erziehungsministerium
in Rio de Janeiro
Sonnenschutz mit beweglichen Storen
Architekten Costa, Niemeyer, Reidy, Leao,
Moreira, Berater Le Corbusier

Bürohaus in Prag
kreuzweiser Grundriss der hohen Trakte
vorbildliche Gesamtdisposition
an der Strasse niedrige Bauten
Architekten Havlicek & Honzik, Prag

Office Buildings

Office buildings planned as a group
Mix of low-slung and tall buildings
Intensive use of available space, and yet spacious
Rockefeller Center building complex, New York
Architects: Reinhard & Hofmeister, Corbett
Harriman & Mac Murray, Hood & Fouilhoux

Ministry of Health & Education
in Rio de Janeiro
Sun protection through movable shades
Architects: Costa, Niemeyer, Reidy, Leao,
Moreira, Advisor: Le Corbusier

Office building in Prague
Transverse floor plan for the higher wings
Exemplary overall layout
on a street of low buildings
Architects: Havlicek & Honzik, Prague

Das Schulzimmer

Pavillon-Schule in Los Angeles
Querlüftung der Klassenräume
beidseitige Beleuchtung
mit hochliegenden Fenstern
grosse Fenster-Schiebewand gegen Garten
Architekt Richard J. Neutra, Los Angeles

Klassenzimmer
freie Bestuhlung, Querlüftung
doppelseitige Belichtung
Ausführung einfach und unproblematisch
Architekten Perkins & Will, Chicago

Klassenzimmer im 1. Stock
doppelseitige Belichtung und Querlüftung
Möglichkeiten im mehrstöckigen Bau
die Vorteile der Pavillonschulen zu erreichen
Architekten Kräher & Bosshard, Zürich

The Classroom

Pavilion school in Los Angeles
Cross ventilation of classrooms
Daylight from both sides
through high-set windows
Large sliding glass doors give onto a garden
Architect: Richard J. Neutra, Los Angeles

Classroom
Freely placed seating, cross-ventilation
Daylight from both sides
Simple and unproblematic execution
Architects: Perkins & Will, Chicago

Second-floor classroom
Daylight from both sides and cross-ventilation
Possibilities in a multistory building
of achieving the advantages of pavilion schools
Architects: Kräher & Bosshard, Zurich

Bildungsstätten

Gewerbeschule Bern
Baukörper auf Stützen gestellt
darunter Pausenhalle
klare, saubere Gestaltung
Architekt Hans Brechbühler, Bern

Bauhaus, Hochschule für Gestaltung
Gebäude in Dessau (erbaut 1926)
klare Trennung der Funktionen
Werkstätten, Studentenateliers, Unterrichtsäle
Architekt Walter Gropius
jetzt Cambridge (U.S.A.)

Wohn- & Ausbildungszentrum ‚Taliesin West'
von Frank Lloyd Wright bei Phoenix, Arizona
Ansicht des Flügels mit dem Zeichensaal
einfache Holzkonstruktion mit Klappwänden

Educational Institutions

Gewerbeschule Bern (Vocational School)
Building set atop pillars
with recreation hall underneath
Clear, clean-lined design
Architect: Hans Brechbühler, Bern

Bauhaus, Hochschule für Gestaltung
(College of Design)
Building in Dessau (built 1926)
Clear separation of functions
Workshops, student studios, lecture halls
Architect: Walter Gropius, now in Cambridge
(USA)

Taliesin West Residential & Training Center
by Frank Lloyd Wright, near Phoenix, Arizona
View of wing with drafting studio
Simple timber construction with hinged walls

Hochschulen

Universitätsgebäude in Miami (USA)
Blick vom Treppenhaus
auf die Sonnenschutz-Galerien
vor den Unterrichtsräumen
Architekt Robert Law Weed und Mitarbeiter

Gebäude d. Technischen Hochschule Chicago
Stahlskelett in differenzierten Proportionen
vorzügliche ästhetische Wirkung
durch äusserste Einfachheit
Architekt Ludwig Mies van der Rohe, Chicago

Zeichensaal im Maschinenlaboratorium
der Eidgen. Technischen Hochschule Zürich
beidseitige Belichtung, Querlüftung
sichtbares Stahlskelett
Architekt Alfred Roth, Zürich

Universities

University building in Miami (USA)
View from staircase
of sun-protected galleries
giving onto the classrooms
Architect: Robert Law Weed and Associates

Illinois Institute of Technology, Chicago
Steel skeleton with differentiated proportions
Splendid aesthetic impact
through extreme simplicity
Architect: Ludwig Mies van der Rohe, Chicago

Drafting studio in the machine laboratory
at the Eidgenössische Technische Hochschule
Zurich (Federal Technical University)
Light from both sides, cross-ventilation
Visible steel skeleton
Architect: Alfred Roth, Zurich

Forms in planning and architecture

Bauten für die Heilkunde

Tuberkulose-Sanatorium in Waukegan
sorgfältige architektonische Ausbildung
vorgelagerte Liegeterrassen zum weiten Park
Architekten William A. Ganster
und William L. Pereira

Museum of Modern Art, New York

Kantonsspital und Universitätsklinik Zürich
organische Eingliederung der Baukörper
in den vorhandenen Park
aufgelockerte, doch stark gebund. Disposition
Architektengemeinschaft Arter & Risch, Haefeli
Moser, Steiger, Landolt, Leuenberger &
Flückiger, Schütz, Weideli, Dr. Fietz

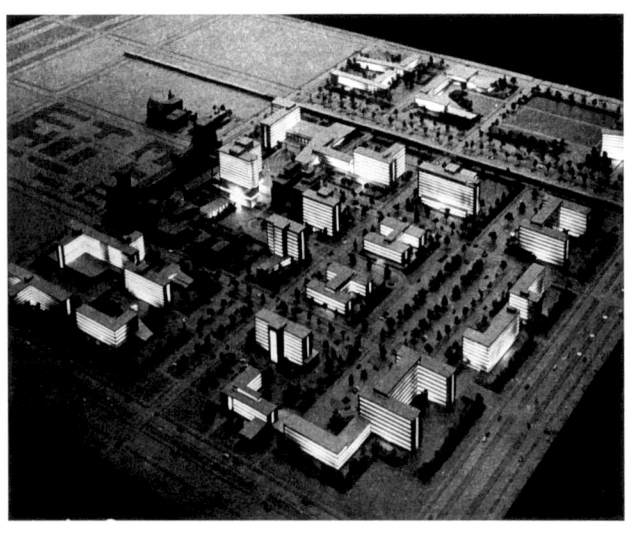

Ausschnitt medizinisches Quartier Chicago
alle möglichen Institute umfassend:
Spitäler, Kliniken, Unterrichtsanstalten
Architekten Holabird & Root & Burges;
Sargent & Lundy, Engineers; Pace Associates
Perkins & Will; Schweikher und Elting;
Naess und Murphy

Medical Buildings

Tuberculosis sanatorium in Waukegan
Carefully chosen architectural form
Projecting sun terraces overlooking expansive park
Architects: William A. Ganster and William L. Pereira

Canton Hospital and University Medical Center, Zurich
Organic insertion of building volumes into existing park
Loose but closely integrated layout
Architects' cooperative: Arter & Risch, Haefeli, Moser, Steiger, Landolt, Leuenberger & Flückiger, Schütz, Weideli, Dr. Fietz

Partial view of medical quarter in Chicago encompassing every conceivable institution: hospitals, clinics, educational facilities
Architects: Holabird & Root & Burges; Sargent & Lundy, Engineers; Pace Associates, Perkins & Will; Schweikher and Elting; Naess and Murphy

Bauten in Eisenbeton

Kirche des Southern College, Florida
Konstruktion in Eisenbeton
neuartiger plastischer Ausdruck
Architekt Frank Lloyd Wright, Talisien

Verwaltungsgebäude in Racine
Konstruktion des Hauptraumes
Eisenbetonpilze
Licht durch die Glasoberlichter
Architekt Frank Lloyd Wright, Talisien

Magazingebäude
Eisenbetonschale von 3 cm Stärke
10,5 x 21 Meter
harmonische Erscheinung einer
originellen technischen Konzeption
Konstrukteur Ing. Pier Luigi Nervi, Rom

Reinforced Concrete Buildings

Church of the Southern College, Florida
Building with reinforced concrete
Modern sculptural expression
Architect: Frank Lloyd Wright, Taliesin

Administration building in Racine
Structure of the main hall
Reinforced concrete "mushroom" supports
Light through glass skylights
Architect: Frank Lloyd Wright, Taliesin

Warehouse building
Reinforced concrete shell 3 cm thick
10.5 × 21 meters
Harmonious appearance of an
originally purely technical concept
Design: engineer Pier Luigi Nervi, Rome

Forms in planning and architecture

Beton-Bauelemente

Ausstellungshalle in Turin
90 Meter Spannweite
mit ca. 400 vorfabrizierten Beton-Elementen überwölbt
Leuchtstoffröhren an Unterseite der Rippen
Konstrukteur Ing. Pier Luigi Nervi, Rom

Vorfabrizierte Binder
vorgespannter Eisenbeton
Spannweite 20 m bei 5,70 m Binderabstand
Formgebung nach statischen
und funktionellen Grundsätzen
Hersteller Vobag AG. Zürich

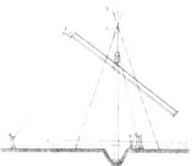

Lokomotiv-Remise
aus vorfabrizierten Tragelementen
in Eisenbeton mit 150 m Durchmesser
Konstrukteur Ing. Bernard Laffaille, Paris

Concrete Construction Elements

Exhibition hall in Turin
90 m span vaulted with approx. 400
prefabricated concrete elements
Fluorescent tubes on the underside of the ribs
Design: engineer Pier Luigi Nervi, Rome

Prefabricated trusses
made of prestressed reinforced concrete
Span width of 20 m with 5.7 m truss spacing
Formal design according to structural engineering
and functional principles
Manufacturer: Vobag AG, Zurich

Locomotive depot
made of prefabricated supporting elements
in reinforced concrete with 150 m diameter
Design: engineer Bernard Laffaille, Paris

Brücken

Rossgraben-Brücke
Kastenträger (Dreigelenkbogen) Eisenbeton
Spannweite 82 Meter
Konstrukteur Ing. Robert Maillart

Bronx-Whitestone-Brücke New York
Hängebrücke mit bemerkenswerter
Konstruktion von Fahrbahn und Aufhängung
Konstrukteur O. H. Ammann, Chefingenieur;
Allston Dona, Entwurfsingenieur;
Aymar Embuny II, Architekt

Schwandbach-Brücke
Stabbogen in Eisenbeton
neuartige Konstruktion, gebogene Fahrbahn
Spannweite 37,40 Meter
Konstrukteur Ing. Robert Maillart

Bridges

Rossgraben Bridge
Reinforced concrete box girders (pin-jointed arch)
Span of 82 m
Design: engineer Robert Maillart

Bronx-Whitestone Bridge, New York
Suspension bridge noteworthy for
design of roadway and suspension system
Design: O. H. Ammann, chief engineer;
Allston Dona, design engineer;
Aymar Embuny II, architect

Schwandbach Bridge
Reinforced concrete tied-arch bridge
Novel design with curving roadway
Span of 37.4 m
Design: engineer Robert Maillart

Hochspannungs-Leitungsmasten

150 kV Freileitung d. Kraftwerke Oberhasli AG.
Gittermasten aus Profileisen
Die Schönheit der Technik
neben den Naturschönheiten
Konstruktion Bernische Kraftwerke, Bern

Nufenenleitung, 150 kV
verspannter Tragmast
mit ausbetonierten Stahlrohren
ausserordentliche Leichtigkeit und Eleganz
Konstruktion Motor-Columbus AG. Baden

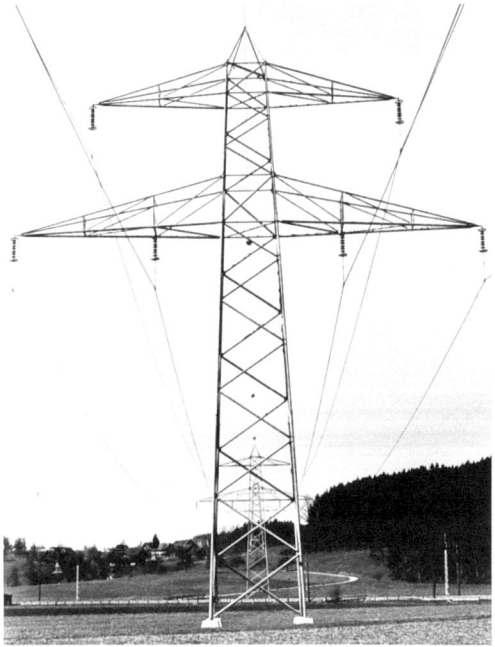

Hochspannungsleitung Amsteg-Mettlen
380 kV, ausbetonierte Stahlrohre
Konstruktion Motor-Columbus AG. Baden

High-Voltage Power Line Masts

150 kV aerial line from Oberhasli AG power plant
Pylon of sectional iron
The beauty of technology
next to the beauty of nature
Design: Bernische Kraftwerke, Bern

Nufenen power line, 150 kV
suspension tower
with concrete-lined steel pipes
Extraordinary lightness and elegance
Design: Motor-Columbus AG, Baden

Amsteg-Mettlen high-voltage power line
380 kV, concrete-lined steel pipes
Design: Motor-Columbus AG, Baden

Stileinheit der Technik

Staudamm am Tennessee
zur Elektrizitätserzeugung u. Fluss-Schiffahrt
klare Disposition
vernünftige Formgebung bis ins Detail

Hochspannungsleitung
der TVA-Kraftleitung
vorbildlich gestalteter Gittermast
in Stahlprofilen

Generatorenhalle im Tennessee-Flusstal
Umhüllung aller mechanischen Teile
in guten Proportionen und Winkeln

Stylistic Unity in Technology

Dam in Tennessee
for electricity generation and river navigation
Clear layout
Sensible design down to the last detail

High-voltage power line
for TVA power supply
Exemplary design of pylon
with sectional steel

Generator hall in Tennessee River Valley
All mechanical parts enclosed
with good proportions and angles

Forms in planning and architecture

Vorfabrizierte Bauten

Montagehaus
britisches Erzeugnis
Dreizimmer-Typ
Stahlskelett, Eternit-Aussenrandverkleidung
Entwürfe Architektengruppe Acron

Holzkonstruktion
in Polygonalsystem
aus regelmässigen Querschnitten
für 100 m² überdeckte Fläche
sind ca. 2,2 m³ Holz nötig
Erfinder Ing. Robert Le Ricolais, Paris

Platten auf Stockwerkhöhe
Stahlblech isoliert
in Stahlkonstruktion an
Markthalle und Volkshaus in Clichy-Paris
Architekten Beaudouin & Lods, Paris

Prefabricated Buildings

Prefabricated house
British product
Three-room type
Steel skeleton, cement asbestos siding
Designs: Acron architects group

Wooden structure
using polygonal system
of regular cross-sections
Approx. 2.2 m² of wood are needed to
span an area of 100 m²
Inventor: engineer Robert Le Ricolais, Paris

Story-height slabs
insulated with sheet steel
in a steel structure for a
market hall and community center in Clichy-Paris
Architects: Beaudouin & Lods, Paris

Norm-Bestandteile

Brief- und Milchkasten
kombiniertes Norm-System
zweckmässige, vernünftige Lösung
Hersteller Metallbau AG. Zürich-Albisrieden

Kellerfenster
Stahlkonstruktion mit Mäusegitter
einfache, solide Norm-Ausführung
Hersteller Metallbau AG. Zürich-Albisrieden

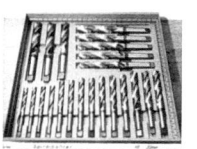

Stahlschränke
Schubladen auf Rollen
mit verschiedensten Innenteilungen
nach Bedürfnis kombinierbar
Hersteller Metallbau AG. Zürich-Albisrieden

Standard Components

Letter and milk boxes
Combined standard system
Functional, sensible solution
Manufacturer: Metallbau AG, Zurich-Albisrieden

Basement window
Steel construction with close-meshed grid
Simple, solid standard design
Manufacturer: Metallbau AG, Zurich-Albisrieden

Steel cabinets
Drawers on wheels
with a wide variety of inner separators
Can be combined as needed
Manufacturer: Metallbau AG, Zurich-Albisrieden

Kücheneinrichtungen

Einbau-Küche
Zusammenbau verschiedener Apparate
darüber durchgehende Abdeckung
mit rostfreiem Chromnickelstahl
Hersteller Walter Franke Aarburg

Geschirr- und Textilwaschmaschine
mit auswechselbarer Trommel
erzielt müheloses Abwaschen
erspart eine Waschküche
Modell ‚Thor' Verkauf Busco AG. Zürich

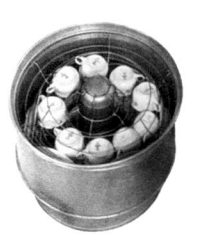 

Elektrischer Kochherd
wohlüberlegte Durchbildung aller Teile
gute Schalter
gutes Markenzeichen, gut plaziert
Hersteller Sursee-Werke AG. Sursee

Kitchen Furnishings

Built-in kitchen
Assemblage of various appliances
under a continuous countertop
With stainless chromium-nickel steel
Manufacturer: Walter Franke, Aarburg

Dish and clothes washer
with replaceable drum
Effortless washing
No need for a laundry room
Model: Thor
Sold by: Busco AG, Zurich

Electric stove
Well-considered design of all parts
Good switches
Good logo, well placed
Manufacturer: Sursee-Werke AG, Sursee

Sanitäre Apparate

Toilette mit Abstellfläche
Ausguss
neue keramische Formen, Neo-Armaturen
Modelle A. K. Z. Zürich
Hersteller AG. für Keramische Industrie, Laufen
Armaturen: Karrer, Weber & Co. Unterkulm

Behälter für flüssige Seife
Messing verchromt
zweckmässige Durchbildung aus der Funktion
Hersteller Nyffenegger & Co. Zürich-Oerlikon

Wandtoiletten im Operationssaal
des Kantonsspitals Zürich
Toiletten: AG. für Keramische Industrie, Laufen
Modelle A.K.Z. Zürich
Armaturen: Karrer, Weber & Co. Unterkulm

Bathroom Fittings

Sink with shelf area
Basin
New ceramic forms, neo-faucets
Models: A. K. Z., Zurich
Manufacturer: AG für Keramische Industrie, Laufen
Faucets: Karrer, Weber & Co., Unterkulm

Dispenser for liquid soap
Chrome-plated brass
Practical form derived from function
Manufacturer: Nyffenegger & Co., Zurich-Oerlikon

Wall sinks in operating room
of Canton Hospital, Zurich
Sinks: AG für Keramische Industrie, Laufen
Models: A. K. Z., Zurich
Faucets: Karrer, Weber & Co., Unterkulm

Sanitäre Armaturen

Wolgensinger, Zürich

Wandbatterie
geschmeidige, elegante Form
eines kleinen, aber wichtigen
architektonischen Details
Hersteller Karrer, Weber & Co. AG. Unterkulm

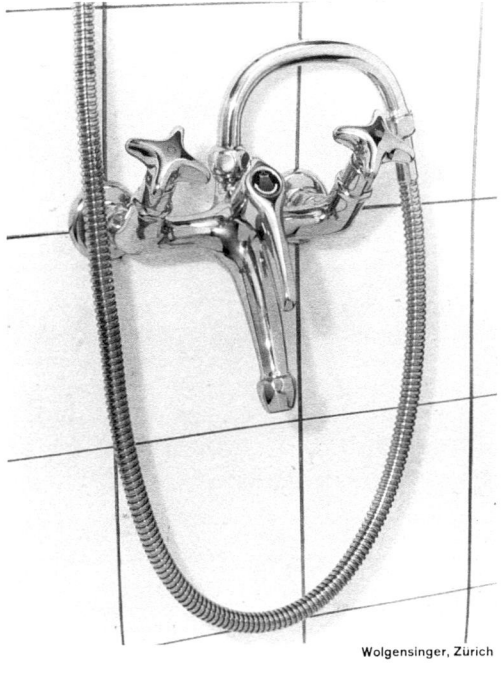

Wolgensinger, Zürich

Badebatterie
Neo-Armatur in
zweckmässiger Gestaltung unter
Mitarbeit eines Architekten
Hersteller Karrer, Weber & Co. AG. Unterkulm

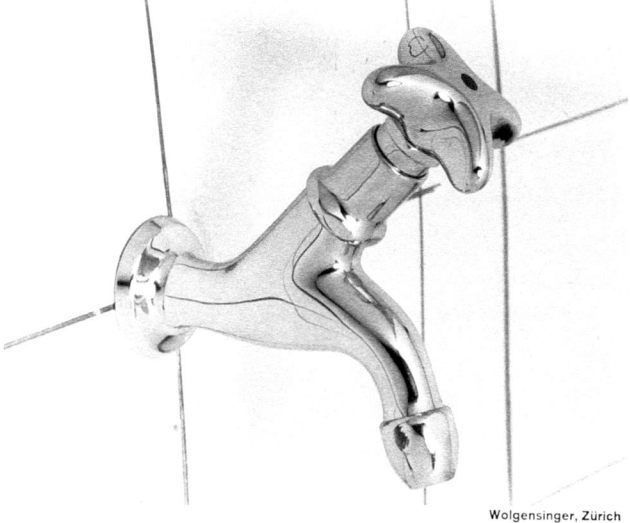

Wolgensinger, Zürich

Auslaufhahn
technisch einwandfreie Durchbildung
Schrägstellung des Sterngriffes
aus der Funktion entwickelt
Hersteller Karrer, Weber & Co. AG. Unterkulm

Bathroom Faucets

Wall mixer
Sleek, elegant form
for a small, yet important
architectural detail
Manufacturer: Karrer, Weber & Co., AG, Unterkulm

Bath mixer
Neo-faucet in a practical design
conceived in collaboration with
an architect
Manufacturer: Karrer, Weber & Co., AG, Unterkulm

Outlet tap
Technically perfected form
Tilted star handle
developed out of the function
Manufacturer: Karrer, Weber & Co., AG, Unterkulm

Forms in home fittings and furnishings

Lichtschalter und Stecker

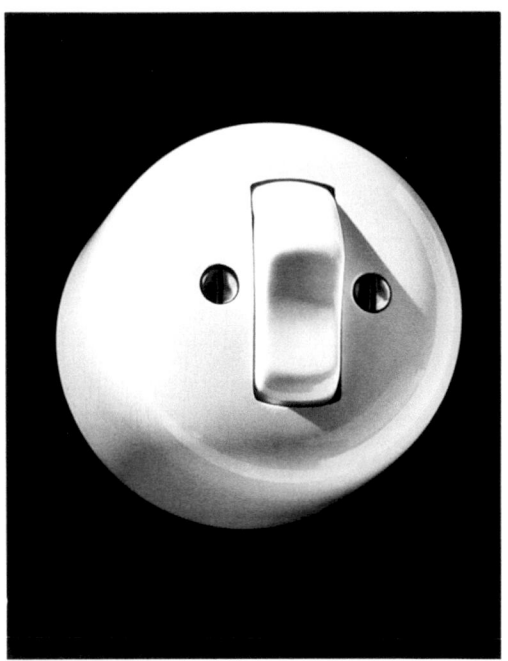

Kippschalter aus Kunstharz
mit neuartigem Schalterknopf
vielleicht die endgültige Form
eines elektrischen Lichtschalters überhaupt
Hersteller Adolf Feller AG. Horgen

Lichtschalter und Steckdose in Kunstharz
für Unterputzmontage
einwandfreie Formgebung
neuartiger Schalterknopf zum Kippen
Hersteller Adolf Feller AG. Horgen

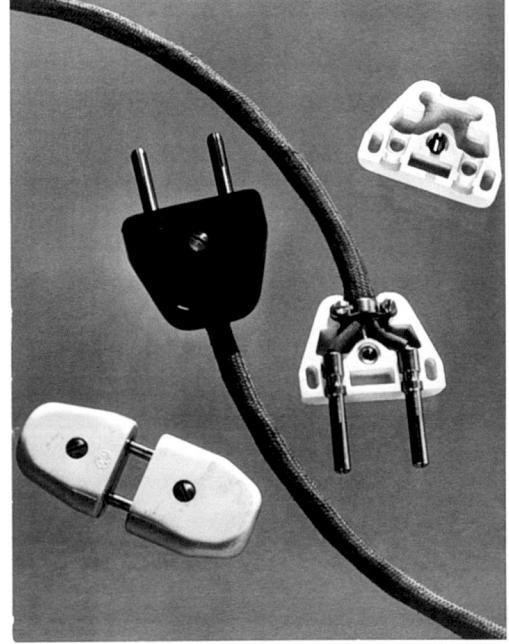

Lichtstecker
neue Form in Kunstharz
möglichst kantenlos
gute, griffige Durchbildung
Hersteller Adolf Feller AG. Horgen

Light Switches and Plugs

Rocker switch of synthetic resin
with new kind of switch head
Perhaps the definitive form
of an electric light switch
Manufacturer: Adolf Feller AG, Horgen

Light switch and socket of synthetic resin
for in-wall mounting
Consummate design
New kind of rocking switch
Manufacturer: Adolf Feller AG, Horgen

Lamp plugs
New form in synthetic resin
Edges rounded as much as possible
Good design with good grip
Manufacturer: Adolf Feller AG, Horgen

Pendel-Leuchten

Indirekt-Leuchte
für Büro, Laden, Wohnraum
Untersicht weiss-matt aufgehellt
vom Reflektor angeleuchtet
Modell Alluminium-Licht AG. Zürich

Indirektleuchte
aus Aluminium, eingebauter Spiegelreflektor
Entwurf Architekt Max Bill SWB, Zürich
Hersteller B.A.G. Turgi

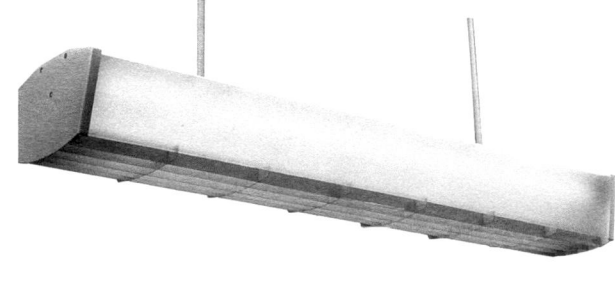

Lampe mit Leuchtstoffröhre
seitlich Mattglas
nach unten Abdeckung mit weissen Lamellen
Verhinderung jeder Blendwirkung
Modell Alluminium-Licht AG. Zürich

Hanging Lamps

Indirect lighting
for office, shop, living space
Underside matte white
illuminated by reflector
Model: Alluminium-Licht AG, Zurich

Lamp for indirect lighting
made of aluminum, built-in mirror reflector
Design: architect Max Bill SWB, Zurich
Manufacturer: B.A.G., Turgi

Lamp with fluorescent tube
Matte glass sides
Underside with white lamellas
prevents glare
Model: Alluminium-Licht AG, Zurich

Forms in home fittings and furnishings

Tischlampen

Tischlampe
allseitig drehbar
weit auskragend, gut ausbalanciert
Hersteller Aluminium-Licht AG. Zürich

Leichte Tischlampe
Pergament oder Papier
auf Hartstäben
Entwurf Isamu Naguchi, New York
Verkauf Wohnbedarf Zürich und S. Jehle Basel

Finsler, Zürich

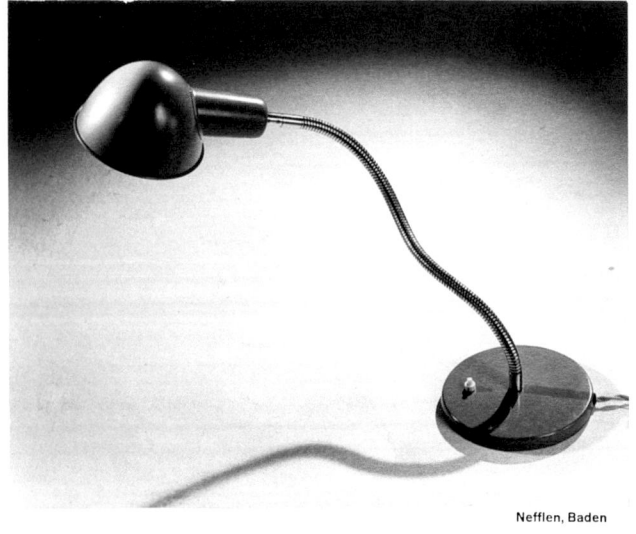

Nefflen, Baden

Tischlampe
allseitig beweglich
einfache, klare Form
Hersteller BAG Turgi

Table Lamps

Desk lamp
rotatable in all directions
Well balanced to lean out far without tipping
Manufacturer: Alluminium-Licht AG, Zurich

Lightweight table lamp
Parchment or paper
on rigid rods
Design: Isamu Naguchi, New York
Sold by: Wohnbedarf, Zurich, and S. Jehle, Basel

Desk lamp
Can be moved in all directions
Simple, clear-cut form
Manufacturer: BAG, Turgi

Kombinations-Tische

Satz-Tische aus 4 Teilen
beliebig kombinierbar
zusammenstellbar auf die Grösse
eines Elements
Entwurf Institute of Design, Chicago

Institute of Design, Chicago

Caruelle-Tisch
in der Höhe verstellbar
Tischblatt teilweise drehbar
als Krankentisch, Lesetisch etc. benutzbar
Hersteller Embru-Werke AG. Rüti-Zürich

Herdeg, Zürich

Ess- und Teetisch
einklappbare Beine aus Stahlrohr
gute Verspannung der Füsse
Entwurf Charles Eames, Venice (California)

Combination Tables

Set of four tables
Can be combined in multiple ways
Stackable to the size of a single element
Design: Institute of Design, Chicago

Caruelle table
Height adjustable
Tabletop tilts partially
For use as bedside table for the bedridden, reading table, etc.
Manufacturer: Embru-Werke AG, Rüti-Zurich

Dining and tea table
Collapsible tubular steel legs
Good tensioning of legs
Design: Charles Eames, Venice (CA)

Forms in home fittings and furnishings

Serviertische

Servierbrett mit Füssen
in vollem Zustand zusammenklappbar und
verstellbar
leichte Holzkonstruktion

Doppelte Abstellfläche
Bugholz und Sperrholz
daher sehr leicht
Entwurf Architekten Alvar und Aino Aalto,
Helsinki

Servierboy mit grossen Rädern
doppelte Abstellfläche
Flaschenkorb
Entwurf Architekten Aino und Alvar Aalto,
Helsinki

Serving Tables

Serving tray with feet
Can be folded and adjusted
while loaded
Lightweight wood construction

Double usable surface
Bentwood and plywood
and thus very light in weight
Design: architects Alvar and Aino Aalto,
Helsinki

Serving cart with large wheels
Double usable surface
Bottle basket
Design: architects Aino and Alvar Aalto,
Helsinki

Teetische

Zusammenklappbarer Teetisch
auf kleinstem Raum unterzubringen
einfache Montage
Entwurf Architekt Hans Bellmann SWB, Zürich
Modell Wohnbedarf Zürich und S. Jehle Basel

Wolgensinger, Zürich

Teetisch
Winkeleisenrahmen mit Kristallglas
einfachste Ausführungsmöglichkeit
Wirkung durch gute Proportion
Hersteller Edgewood Furniture Comp. Inc.
New York

Teetisch
quer gesägter Baumstamm
auf Eisenfüssen
Wirkung durch unbearbeitetes Material
Entwurf Charlotte Perriand, Paris

Tea Tables

Foldable tea table
Fits into the smallest of spaces
Simple assembly
Design: architect Hans Bellmann, SWB, Zurich
Model: Wohnbedarf, Zurich, and S. Jehle, Basel

Tea table
Angle iron frame with cut-glass tabletop
Simplest execution option
High impact through good proportions
Manufacturer: Edgewood Furniture Comp. Inc.,
New York

Tea table
Cross-section of tree trunk
on iron feet
High impact through rough, unprocessed material
Design: Charlotte Perriand, Paris

Sperrholz- und Schichtholz-Stühle

Schichtholz-Stuhl
dreidimensionale Neuformung
Sitz und Rücklehne ein Stück
leicht federnd
Hersteller Möbelfabrik Horgen-Glarus, Glarus

Heiniger, Zürich

Einfacher Stuhl
Bugholz und Sperrholz
leichte saubere Konstruktion
Möbelfabrik Horgen-Glarus

Finsler, Zürich

Hocker
in grossen Quantitäten stapelbar
Bugholz mit Sperrholzplatte
Entwurf Architekten Aino und Alvar Aalto
Helsinki
Vertrieb Wohnbedarf AG. Zürich und S. Jehle
Basel

Plywood and Laminated Wood Chairs

Laminated wood chair
Three-dimensional reshaping
Seat and backrest made of one piece
Slightly springy
Manufacturer: Horgen-Glarus furniture factory, Glarus

Simple chair
Bentwood and plywood
Light, clean design
Manufacturer: Horgen-Glarus furniture factory

Stools
Can be stacked in great quantities
Bentwood with plywood top
Design architects: Aino and Alvar Aalto, Helsinki
Sold by: Wohnbedarf AG, Zurich, and S. Jehle, Basel

Sitzmöbel mit Gurten

Esszimmer-Stuhl
Gurtenbespannung
aus Brettern gleicher Stärke konstruiert
Entwurf Jens Risom, Modell Knoll Associates
New York

Finsler, Zürich

Ruhe-Sessel
mit Gurtenbespannung
Entwurf Jens Risom, Modell Knoll Associates
New York
Vertrieb Wohnbedarf AG. Zürich und S. Jehle
Basel

Finsler, Zürich

Liegestuhl
aus Bugholz
mit Gurtenbespannung
Entwurf Architekten Aino und Alvar Aalto
Helsinki

Finsler, Zürich

Woven-Strap Chairs

Dining room chair
Seat and back of woven straps
of uniform width
Design: Jens Rison
Model: Knoll Associates, New York

Easy chair
with continuous seat and back of woven straps
Design: Jens Rison
Model: Knoll Associates, New York
Sold by: Wohnbedarf AG, Zurich, and S. Jehle, Basel

Lounge chair
of bentwood
with woven straps
Design: architects Aino and Alvar Aalto, Helsinki

Forms in home fittings and furnishings

Sessel

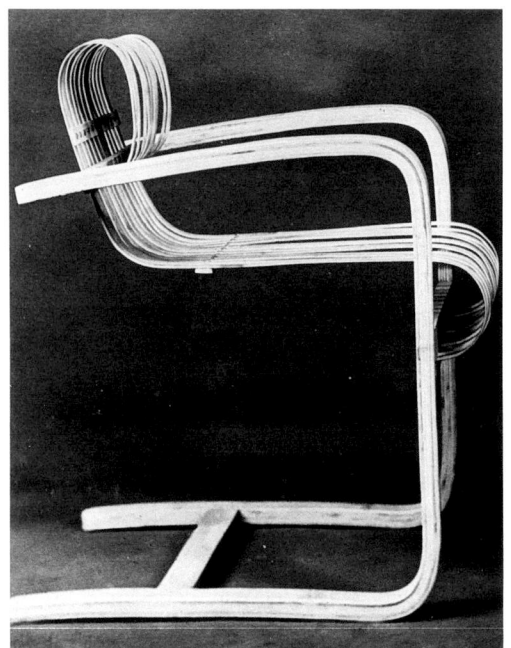

Holz-Sessel
Gestell Schichtholz
Sitzfläche in federnden Holzplatten
japanische Herstellung und Technik
Modell Charlotte Perriand, Paris

Sessel
Holz mit Lederpolstern
sorgfältige formale Gestaltung
Entwurf Architekt Finn Juhl, Kopenhagen
Hersteller Schreinermeister Niels Vodder
Kopenhagen

Schichtholzsessel
mit Stahlrohrgestell
Rücklehne leicht beweglich
elegante, gutgeformte Lösung
Modell Architekt Charles Eames, Venice, Cal.

Armchairs

Wooden armchair
Laminated wood frame
Seat of springy wooden boards
Japanese production and technology
Model: Charlotte Perriand, Paris

Armchair
Wood with leather cushions
Carefully considered formal design
Design: architect Finn Juhl, Copenhagen
Manufacturer: master joiner Niels Vodder, Copenhagen

Laminated wood chair
with tubular steel frame
Backrest gives slightly
Elegant, well-formed solution
Model: architect Charles Eames, Venice, CA

Ruhe-Sessel

Fauteuil für hohe Ansprüche
Stahlbandkonstruktion verchromt
flexible Lederpolster auf Gurten
Entwurf Architekt Ludwig Mïes van der Rohe, Chicago

Zusammenlegbares Modell
aus Holz, Segeltuch, Lederriemen
geringster Materialaufwand
waschbare Segeltuchteile
Vertrieb Wohnbedarf AG. Zürich und Basel

Finsler, Zürich

Schalenförmige Sperrholzkonstruktion
Gummipolsterung mit Stoffüberzug
flexible Einzelkissen
Stahlrohrtragkonstruktion
Entwurf Architekt Eero Saarinen
Vertrieb Knoll Associates, New York

Easy Chairs

Fauteuil for those with discerning tastes
Frame of chrome-plated steel strips
Flexible leather cushions resting on straps
Design: architect Ludwig Mies van der Rohe, Chicago

Foldable model
of wood, sailcloth, leather straps
Minimal materials
Washable sailcloth elements
Sold by: Wohnbedarf AG, Zurich, and Basel

Bowl-shaped plywood seat
Rubber upholstery covered in fabric
Flexible, loose cushions
Tubular steel frame
Design: architect Eero Saarinen
Sold by: Knoll Associates, New York

Forms in home fittings and furnishings

Liegemöbel

Couch
besteht aus 2 gleichen Elementen
4 Sitz- und 4 Rückenpolster
davon eine Partie als Akzent bestickt
ausgeführt in Japan
Modell Charlotte Perriand, Paris

Bett-Couch
Lattenrost federnd
darauf DEA-Matratze mit Federeinlagen
Modell Wohnbedarf Zürich und S. Jehle, Basel

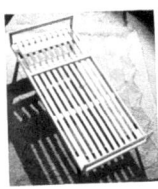

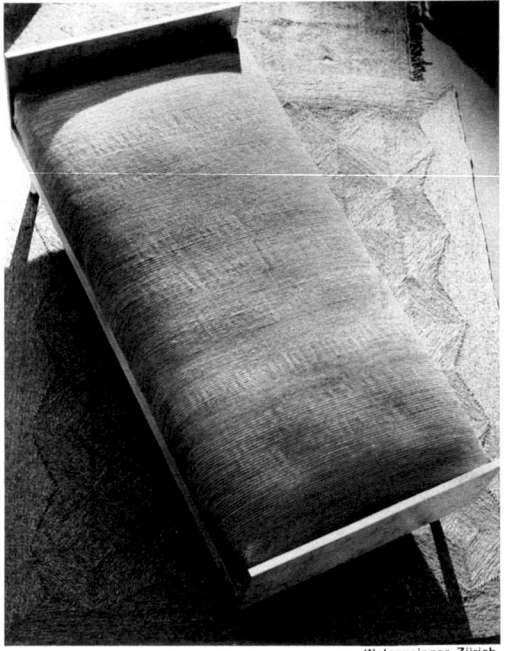

Wolgensinger, Zürich

Bett
Federung aus flexibel eingespannten
Holzleisten
ausgeführt in Japan
Modell Charlotte Perriand, Paris

Beds and Daybeds

Couch
consisting of two uniform elements,
four seat and four back cushions
One section is embroidered as an accent
Executed in Japan
Model: Charlotte Perriand, Paris

Bed-couch
Slatted frame with springs
holding a DEA spring mattress
Model: Wohnbedarf, Zurich, and S. Jehle, Basel

Bed
Flexibly stretched wooden slats
for springiness
Executed in Japan
Model: Charlotte Perriand, Paris

Wohnräume

Wohnraum
mit Einzelmöbeln
handwerkliche Herstellung
Modelle Nauer & Vogel SWB Zürich

Nefflen, Baden

Kinder-Schlaf- und Spielzimmer
Platzsparende Bettenanordnung
ermöglicht grossen Tagesraum
Entwurf Gustav Allert
Hersteller Kooperativa Förbundet,
Möbelavdelningen, Stockholm

Kunstgewerbeschule Zürich

Wohn-Essraum
saubere Möbeltypen
für handwerkliche Serienproduktion
Modelle Genossenschaft Hobel, Zürich

Living Rooms

Living room
with individual furniture pieces
Artisanal production
Models: Nauer & Vogel, SWB Zurich

Children's bed- and playroom
Space-saving bed arrangement
frees up space in the daytime
Design: Gustav Allert
Manufacturer: Kooperativa Förbundet
Möbelavdelningen, Stockholm

Living/dining room
Clean-lined furniture types
for artisanal series production
Models: Genossenschaft Hobel, Zurich

Forms in home fittings and furnishings

Leben im Garten

Planschbecken
Gummi, auf kleinstes Format zusammenlegbar
die Form entsteht durch Füllen mit Wasser
weiche Ränder schützen die Kinder
Hersteller International B. S. Goodrich Co.
Acron (U. S. A.)

Gartenstuhl
Ausführung in gepresstem Aluminium
kann aufeinander gestapelt werden
Modell Dr. Hans Coray SWB Zürich
Hersteller P. & W. Blattmann, Wädenswil

Kunstgewerbeschule Zürich

Heiniger, Zürich

Gartentisch
Füsse aus Rundeisen
Platte aus Eisenblech
sehr leicht, demontierbar
Modell Wilhelm Kienzle SWB Zürich
Hersteller P. & W. Blattmann, Wädenswil

Garden Living

Kiddie pool
Rubber, foldable for compact storage
The form results from filling with water
Child-safe soft rim
Manufacturer: International B.S. Goodrich Co.,
Akron (USA)

Garden chair
Made of extruded aluminum
Can be stacked
Model: Dr. Hans Coray, SWB, Zurich
Manufacturer: P. & W. Blattmann, Wädenswil

Garden table
Legs of iron rod, tabletop of sheet iron
Very lightweight, can be disassembled
Model: Wilhelm Kienzle, SWB, Zurich
Manufacturer: P. & W. Blattmann, Wädenswil

Sicht- und Sonnen-Schutz

Paravent
aus gleichen Elementen
ineinanderklappbar
Modell Architekt Charles Eames, Venice, Cal.

Lamellenstoren
aus verformtem Aluminium, hell lackiert
sehr platzsparend und leicht
in jeder Richtung feststellbar
Hersteller Metallbau AG. Zürich-Albisrieden

Sonnenstoren
aus feinen Holzstäbchen
Ausnutzung der Befestigung zur Belebung
zusammen mit unaufdringlicher Bemalung
japanisches Modell und Ausführung

Privacy and Sun Shades

Folding screen
of uniform elements
Foldable
Model: architect Charles Eames, Venice, CA

Horizontal aluminum venetian blinds
painted in light tone
Extremely space-saving and lightweight
Can be adjusted in all directions
Manufacturer: Metallbau AG, Zurich-Albisrieden

Sun shades
of fine wooden ribs
Use of attachment technique as design feature
animating the surface, together with reserved
painted decor
Japanese model and execution

Montagemöbel

Vielzweck-Gestell
aus verschieden grossen Elementen
mit und ohne Türen
saubere konstruktive Lösungen
Modell Wilhelm Kienzle SWB Zürich
Hersteller Robert Strub SWB Zürich

Engesser, Zürich

Büchergestell
Bretter Buchenholz
Tragkonstruktion Stahlblech
Modell Wilhelm Kienzle SWB Zürich
Hersteller Embru-Werke, Rüti-Zürich

EAM-Gestelle
aufeinanderstellbare Bestandteile
mit und ohne Türen
gute Grundproportion
Hersteller E. & A. Meier, Zürich

Prefabricated Furniture

Multipurpose frame
of variously sized elements
with and without doors
Clean-lined structural solutions
Model: Wilhelm Kienzle, SWB, Zurich
Manufacturer: Robert Strub, SWB, Zurich

Bookcase
Beechwood boards
Sheet-steel frame
Model: Wilhelm Kienzle, SWB, Zurich
Manufacturer: Embru-Werke, Rüti-Zürich

EAM frames
Stackable elements
with and without doors
Good basic proportions
Manufacturer: E. & A. Meier, Zurich

Eindeutige Geräteformen

Sennerei-Kellen aus Holz
traditionelle, handwerksmässige Ausführung
jedes Gerät durch jahrhundertealte
Erfahrung geformt

Korkenzieher
letzte Form eines einfachen Gegenstandes
aus dem Zweck entwickelt
Hersteller Oskar Ruegg, Federnfabrik
Pfäffikon (Schwyz)

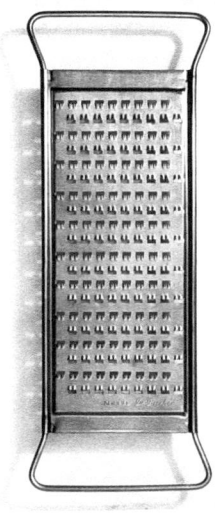 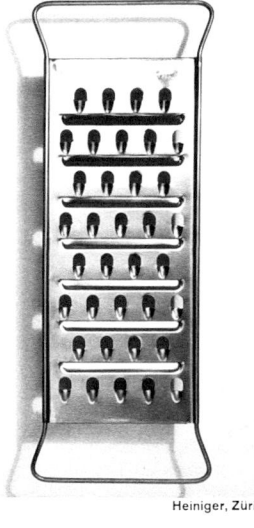

Küchen-Raffeln
aus rostfreiem Stahl
Formgebung aus Funktion und
Fabrikationsmethode
Hersteller Walter Franke, Metallwarenfabrik,
Aarburg

Unambiguous Utensil Forms

Alpine dairy ladles made of wood
Traditional, artisanal design
The form of each utensil is derived from
hundreds of years of experience

Corkscrew
Most recent form of a simple object
developed out of its purpose
Manufacturer: Oskar Ruegg, Federnfabrik
Pfäffikon (Switzerland)

Kitchen graters
made of stainless steel
Form derived from function and
fabrication method
Manufacturer: Walter Franke, metal goods factory,
Aarburg

Forms in home fittings and furnishings

Haushaltgeräte

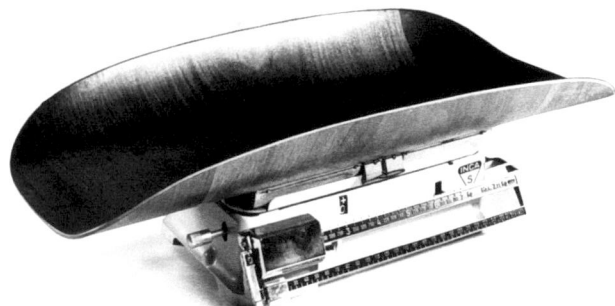

Säuglingswaage
auswechselbare Sperrholzschale
auch als Haushaltwaage benutzbar
Unterbau Spritzguss
Hersteller Injecta AG. Teufenthal

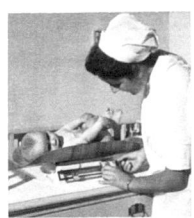

Elektrischer Wärmestrahler
verstellbarer Oberteil
Entwurf Wilhelm Kienzle SWB, Zürich
Hersteller Therma AG. Schwanden

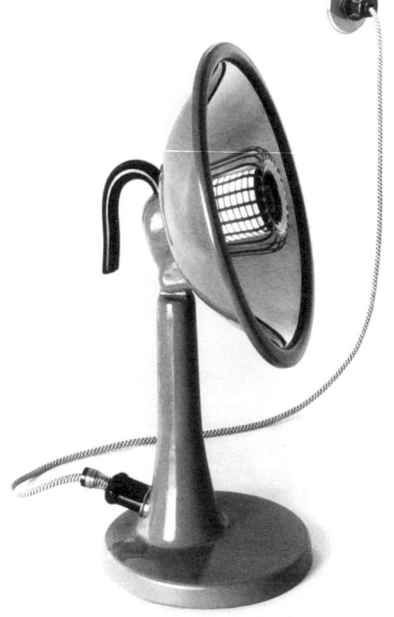

Elektrisches Bügeleisen
mit Wärmeregulierung
und Spezialgriff
Hersteller Therma AG. Schwanden

Household Appliances

Infant scale
Replaceable plywood tray
Can also be used as a household scale
Injection-molded base
Manufacturer: Injecta AG, Teufenthal

Electric radiant heater
Adjustable upper part
Design: Wilhelm Kienzle, SWB, Zurich
Manufacturer: Therma AG, Schwanden

Electric iron
with heat regulator
and special handle
Manufacturer: Therma AG, Schwanden

Küchengeräte

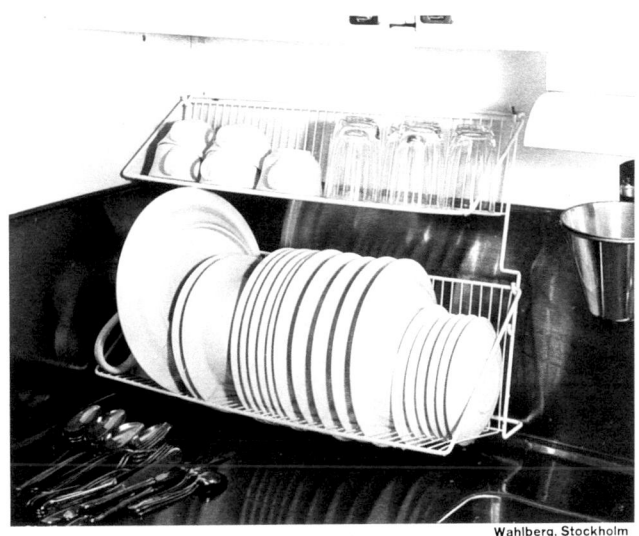

Trockengestell aus Stahl
Berücksichtigung aller praktischen Notwendigkeiten
aushängbare Gitterteile
Modell vom Forschungsinstitut der Heime, Stockholm

Behälter mit Schaufel und Wischer
genannt ‚Kewi'
einfache, praktische Lösung
Entwurf Wilhelm Kienzle SWB, Zürich
Hersteller P. & W. Blattmann, Wädenswil

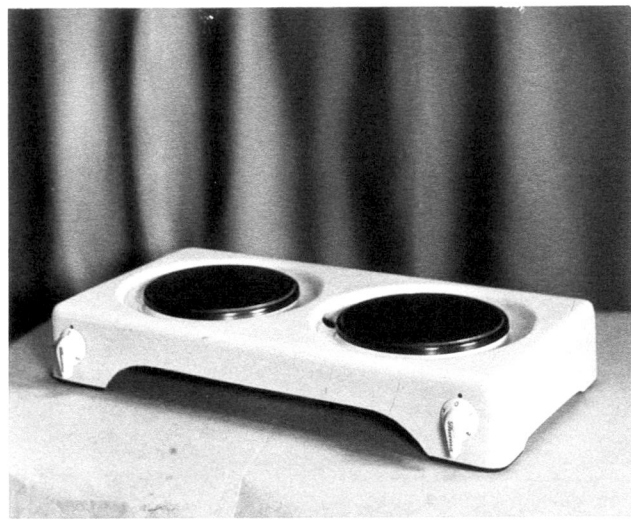

Elektrischer Kochherd
mit Auffangrinne für Ueberkochendes
einfache, zweckmässige Form
Hersteller Therma AG. Schwanden

Kitchen Accessories

Steel dish-drying stand
Consideration of all practical necessities
Removable grids
Model from Household Research Institute, Stockholm

Broom and dustpan holder called "Kewi"
Simple, practical solution
Design: Wilhelm Kienzle, SWB, Zurich
Manufacturer: P. & W. Blattmann, Wädenswil

Electric hotplate
with drip channel to catch spills
Simple, functional form
Manufacturer: Therma AG, Schwanden

Kochgeräte

Rüst- und Brotmesser
rostfreie Stahlklingen,
genietete Griffe aus Rosenholz
schräger Griffansatz in Schnittrichtung
Modelle vom Forschungsinstitut der Heime,
Stockholm

Wahlberg, Stockholm

Bratenschieber mit rostfreien Stahlklingen
Rosenholzgriffe, genietet
Modelle vom Forschungsinstitut der Heime,
Stockholm

Wahlberg, Stockholm

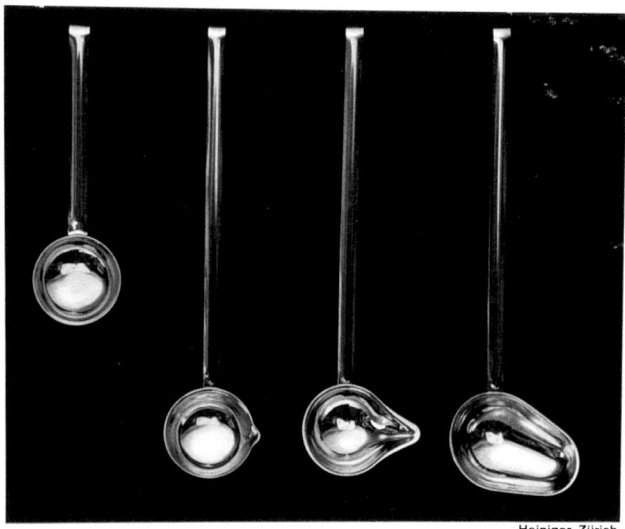

Schöpfkellen
aus rostfreiem Stahl
differenzierte Formen
aus dem Gebrauch entwickelt
Hersteller Walter Franke, Aarburg

Heiniger, Zürich

Kitchen Tools

Paring and bread knifes
Stainless-steel blades,
riveted rosewood handles
Handles slanted in the cutting direction
Models by the Household Research Institute,
Stockholm

Spatulas with stainless-steel blades
Rosewood handles, riveted
Models by the Household Research Institute,
Stockholm

Ladles
of stainless steel
Differentiated forms
developed from use
Manufacturer: Walter Franke, Aarburg

Kochgeschirre

Kanarian, New York

Aluminiumpfannen
Griffe nach der Hand geformt
Schutz gegen Verbrennen der Hand
Entwurf Thomas Lamb, New York

Pfannen für Gas und Elektrisch
emaillierter Stahl
leicht zu reinigen
saubere Wirkung zur direkten Verwendung
auf dem Tisch
Modelle Metallwarenfabrik Zug

Koehli, Zürich

Dean Stone Hugo Steccat, San Francisco

Kochgeschirr in Steinzeug
Deckel, Griff und Fuss ineinanderpassend
kann dadurch aufeinandergestellt werden
kleines Modell für individuellen Service
Modell Heath, Californian Stoneware, Sausalito

Cookware

Aluminum pots and pans
Heatproof handles
shaped to fit the hand
Design: Thomas Lamb, New York

Pots and pans for gas and electric stoves
Enameled steel
Easy to clean
A clean look for direct use on the table
Models: Metallwarenfabrik Zug

Stoneware pots and pans
Lids, handles, and feet made for stacking
Small model for single servings
Model: Heath, Californian Stoneware, Sausalito

Forms in home fittings and furnishings

Porzellan-Gedecke

Essgedeck aus dünnem Porzellan
für den Haushaltsgebrauch
Modell entstand durch eine SWB-Arbeitsgruppe
anlässlich der schweiz. Landesausstellung
Hersteller Porzellanfabrik Langenthal AG.

Tafel-Gedeck
feines, weisses Porzellan mit Goldrand
äusserste Präzision
wohlausgewogene Formen
Entwurf Trude Petri
Hersteller Staatliche Porzellanmanufaktur,
Berlin

Tee-Gedeck
feinstes Porzellan
ausgewogene Formgebung (ca. 1929)
Modelle M. Friedländer
Hersteller Staatliche Porzellanmanufaktur,
Berlin

Porcelain Dishware

Dining service of fine porcelain for household use
Model designed by SWB working group
for the Swiss National Exhibition
Manufacturer: Langenthal AG porcelain factory

Tableware of fine white porcelain with gold border
Extreme precision, balanced forms
Design: Trude Petri
Manufacturer: Staatliche Porzellanmanufactur,
Berlin

Tea service
Finest porcelain
Balanced formal design (c. 1929)
Models: M. Friedländer
Manufacturer: Staatliche Porzellanmanufactur,
Berlin

Kaffee- und Tee-Gedecke

Kaffee-Tee-Gedeck aus feinem Porzellan
für den Haushaltgebrauch
Modell entstanden durch SWB-Arbeitsgruppe
anlässlich der schweiz. Landesausstellung 1939
Hersteller Porzellanfabrik Langenthal AG.

Teegedeck mit typischen Schalentassen
Kanne mit nicht tropfendem Ausguss
handwerksmässige Erzeugung in Ton
Modell H. Haussmann, Werkstatt für Keramik,
Uster

Kaffee- und Teegedeck
kräftige Ausführung in Porzellan
für Restaurants und Hotels
Modell Porzellanfabrik Langenthal AG.

Coffee and Tea Services

Coffee and tea service of fine porcelain
for household use
Model created by SWB working group
for the Swiss National Exhibition in 1939
Manufacturer: Langenthal AG porcelain factory

Tea service with typical shallow cups
Teapot with drip-proof spout
Handcrafted in clay
Model: H. Haussmann, Werkstatt für Keramik, Uster

Coffee and tea service
Sturdy porcelain
for restaurants and hotels
Model: Langenthal AG porcelain factory

Forms in home fittings and furnishings

Trinkgläser

Kunstgewerbeschule Zürich

Kristallglas
in einfachster Form geschliffen
edle Wirkung durch die Schliffe im Boden
Schönheit erzielt durch Verzicht auf Unnötiges
Modell Architekt Adolf Loos

Kunstgewerbeschule Zürich

Gläser
versch. Formen entsprechend dem Gebrauch
harmonische Durchbildung
zweckmässig zum reinigen
Hersteller Compagnie des Cristalleries
de Baccarat, Baccarat

Kunstgewerbeschule Zürich

Trinkgläser und Schalen aus grünem Glas
handwerkliche Verarbeitung
Blasen zur Unterstützung des Material-
und Herstellungscharakters
Vertrieb Wohnbedarf AG. Zürich
und S. Jehle. Basel

Drinking Glasses

Crystal glass
cut into the simplest of forms
Refined look through cut-glass bases
Beauty through renunciation of superfluous details
Model: architect Adolf Loos

Glasses
Various forms according to function
Harmonious design
Easy to clean
Manufacturer: Compagnie des Cristalleries
de Baccarat, Baccarat

Drinking glasses and bowls of green glass
Handcrafted
Bubbles in the glass emphasize the character
of the material and its production
Sold by: Wohnbedarf AG, Zurich, and S. Jehle,
Basel

Kaffee-Kocher

Kaffee-Maschine
4 Filtereinsätze in einer Linie angeordnet
aus der Funktion entwickelte Form
Italienisches Fabrikat ‚La Pavoni'
Modell Architekt Gio Ponti, Milano

Kaffee-Kocher
leicht zu reinigende Form
Griff schützt die Hand vor Verbrennung
britisches Modell
Entwurf F. H. K. Henrion F. S. I. A.
Hersteller F. und F. Electrical Fittings Ltd.

Kaffee- und Teemaschine
Griff so angeordnet,
dass die Hand geschützt ist
leicht in die einzelnen Bestandteile zerlegbar
Entwurf Thomas Lamb, New York

Coffee Makers

Coffee machine
Four filter trays arranged in a row
Form developed from function
Italian make: La Pavoni
Model: architect Gio Ponti, Milan

Coffee maker
Easy-to-clean form
Heatproof handle
British model
Design: F. H. K. Henrion, F.S.I.A.
Manufacturer: F. and F. Electrical Fittings Ltd.

Coffee and tea maker
Handle tilted to protect the hand
Easy to disassemble into constituent parts
Design: Thomas Lamb, New York

Spielzeuge

Kunstgewerbeschule Zürich

Zwei Bären
viereckige Holzplatte in einem Schnitt gesägt
einfachste materialsparende Durchführung
vollkommene Formgebung
Modell Kunstgewerbeschule Zürich

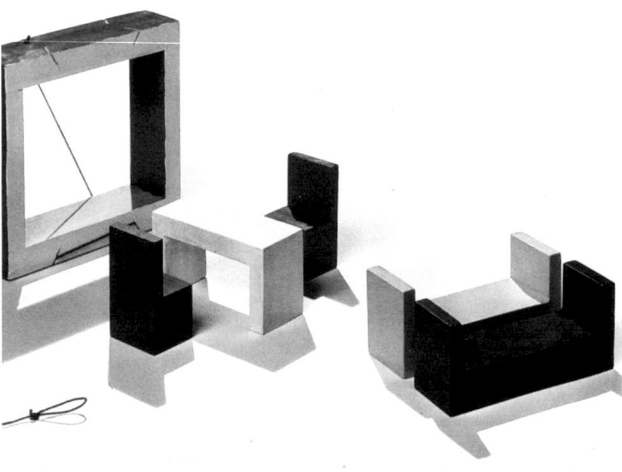

Kunstgewerbeschule Zürich

Baukasten
Möbel, die zusammengepackt werden können
in verschiedenen Farben bemalt
kein Holzabfall bei der Produktion
Modell Kunstgewerbeschule Zürich

Heiniger, Zürich

Spielzeug ‚Bob'
auf der Basis einer technisch
einwandfreien Konstruktion
als Erziehungsmittel
zum eigenen Gestalten
Hersteller Papyria AG. Zürich

Toys

Two bears
Rectangular wooden board sawed in one pass
Simple, material-saving execution
Perfected form
Model: Zurich School of Applied Arts

Construction kit
Furniture that can be packed compactly
Painted in various colors
Produced without wood waste
Model: Zurich School of Applied Arts

"Bob" toy
based on technically
efficient construction
For teaching children
to create their own designs
Manufacturer: Papyria AG, Zurich

Schalen und Behälter

Armour Research Foundation, Chicago

Holzschalen
verschiedene Hölzer, sehr dünn gedrechselt
harmonisches Zusammenspiel von Material
und Form
Entwurf und Ausführung James Prestini,
Armour Research Foundation, Chicago

Kunstgewerbeschule Zürich

Flechtarbeiten
in traditioneller Handwerkstechnik
sehr kultivierte Ausführung
aus den Möglichkeiten der Flechttechnik
entwickelt
Modelle J. A. Schmitter, Helmbrechts
(Oberfranken)

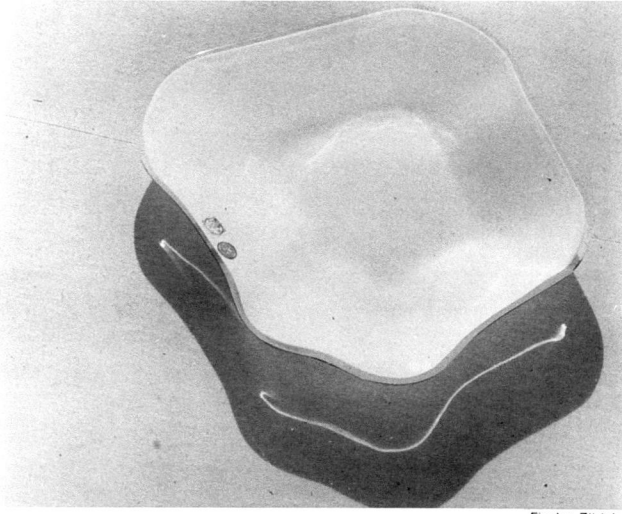

Finsler, Zürich

Früchte-Schale
weisses Ueberfangglas
freie, ausgewogene Form
Entwurf Aino und Alvar Aalto, Helsinki
Modell Artek, Helsinki

Bowls and Containers

Wooden bowls
Various woods, lathed extremely thin
Harmony of material and form
Design and execution: James Prestini,
Armour Research Foundation, Chicago

Basketwork
in traditional handcraftsmanship
Very cultivated execution developed
from the possibilities offered by basket weaving
Models: J. A. Schmitter, Helmbrechts
(Upper Franconia)

Fruit bowl
White flashed glass
Freeform, balanced shape
Design: Aino and Alvar Aalto, Helsinki
Model: Artek, Helsinki

Forms in home fittings and furnishings

Zierformen

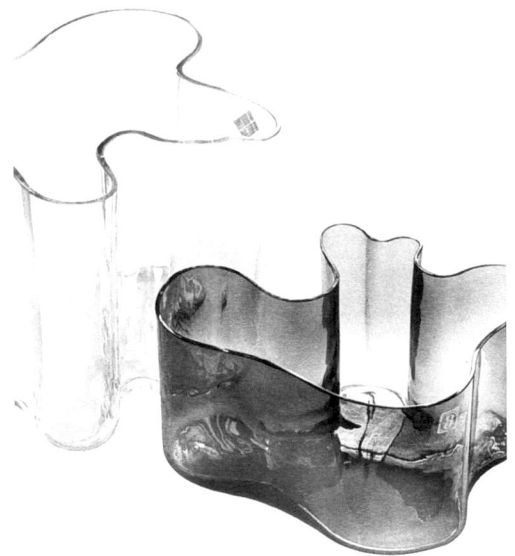

Glasvasen
geschwungene Formen
leichteres Einstellen der Blumen
durch die Einbuchtungen
Modelle von Aino & Alvar Aalto, Helsinki

Finsler, Zürich

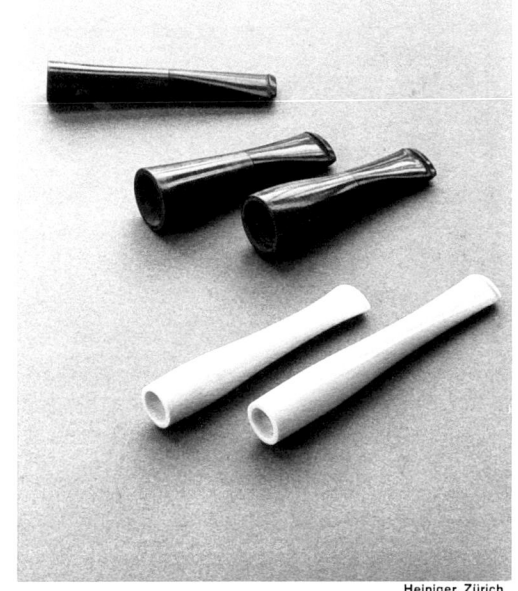

Zigarren- und Zigarettenspitzen
einfache, harmonische Form
dadurch schöne Materialwirkung
Hersteller Odag AG. Zürich

Heiniger, Zürich

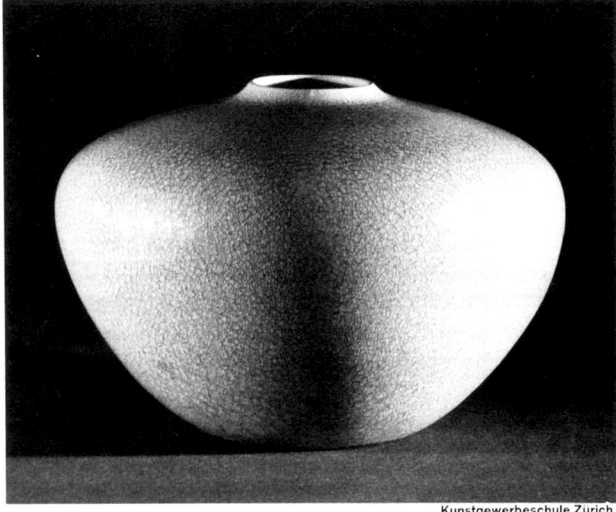

Blumenvase
glasierter Ton
vollendete Form
von E. Haussmann SWB
Keramische Werkstätte, Uster

Kunstgewerbeschule Zurich

Decorative Forms

Glass vases
Curving forms
Easier flower arrangement
thanks to undulating profile
Models by Aino & Alvar Aalto, Helsinki

Cigar and cigarette holders
Simple, harmonious form
brings out the best in the materials
Manufacturer: Odag AG, Zurich

Flower vase
Glazed clay
Consummate form
by E. Haussmann, SWB
Ceramic Workshops, Uster

Toilettengegenstände

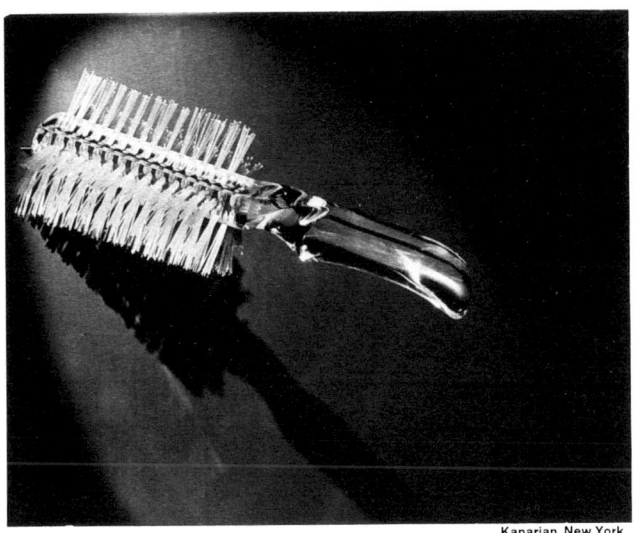

Haarbürste
Plexiglas mit Nylonbürsten
der Hand angepasster Griff
zweckmässige Borstenanordnung
Entwurf Thomas Lamb, New York

Kanarian, New York

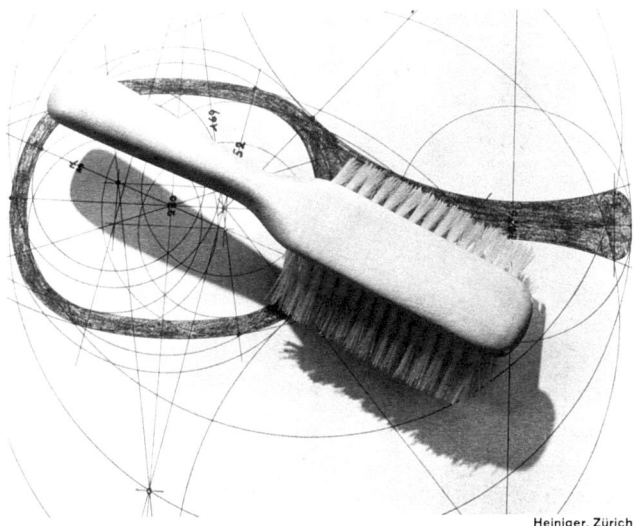

Holzbürste
mit Nylonborsten
handgerechter Griff
Modell Max Bill SWB Zürich
für Bürstenfabrik Walther AG. Oberentfelden

Heiniger, Zürich

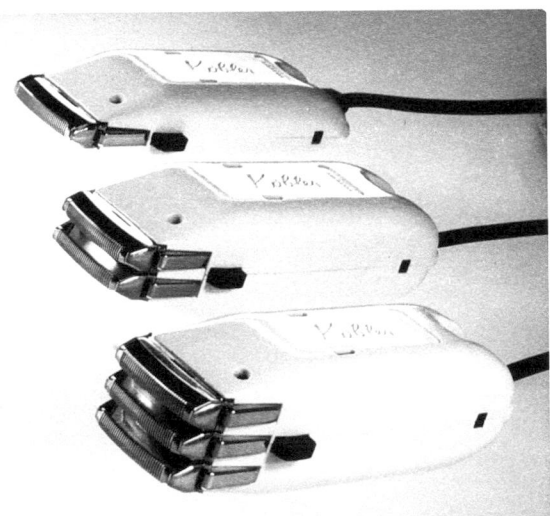

Trockenrasierapparat
auf kleinem Raum in Lederetui verpackbar
3 Typen, verschiedene Zahl von Scherköpfen
Hersteller Kobler & Co. Zürich

Toiletries

Hairbrush
Plexiglas with nylon bristles
Handle adapted to fit the hand
Functional bristle arrangement
Design: Thomas Lamb, New York

Wooden brush
with nylon bristles
Easy-grip handle
Model: Max Bill SWB, Zurich
for Bürstenfabrik Walther AG, Oberentfelden

Dry shaver
fits into compact leather case
Three types, varying number of shaving heads
Manufacturer: Kobler & Co., Zurich

Forms in home fittings and furnishings

Armbanduhren

Compax-Präzisionsuhr
Stopuhr auf Stunden, Minuten, Sekunden
klares, schön geformtes Zifferblatt
Hersteller Universal, Perret & Berthoud S.A.
Genf

Herren-Armbanduhr
harmonische Gesamtwirkung
klares Zifferblatt mit guter Anordnung
Hersteller E. Homberger-Rauschenbach
vorm. International Watch Co., Schaffhausen

Heiniger, Zürich

Damen-Armbanduhr
einfache, klare Durchbildung aller Teile
bei der Gestaltung ist der Schmuckcharakter
berücksichtigt
vorbildliches Zifferblatt
Hersteller E. Homberger-Rauschenbach

Herdeg, Zürich

Wristwatches

Compax precision watch
Stopwatch for hours, minutes, seconds
Clear, pleasingly formed dial
Manufacturer: Universal, Perret & Berthoud S.A., Geneva

Man's watch
Harmonious overall look
Clear dial with good arrangement of elements
Manufacturer: E. Homberger-Rauschenbach,
formerly International Watch Co., Schaffhausen

Woman's watch
Simple, clear design of all parts
The jewelry character is considered in the design
Exemplary dial
Manufacturer: E. Homberger-Rauschenbach

Schmuck

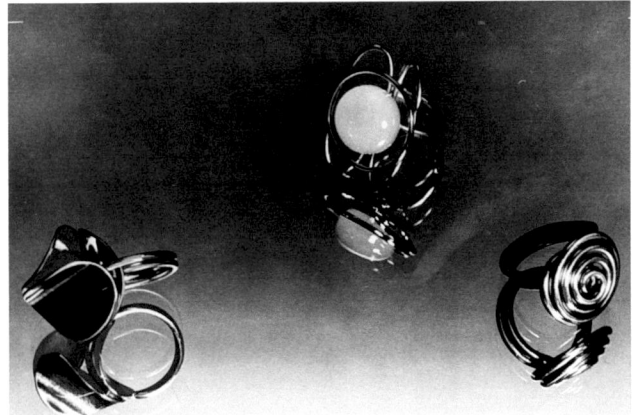

3 Fingerringe
links: aus einem einzigen, ungelöteten Draht
rechts: drei gleiche Platten
aus verschiedenfarbigem Gold
Mitte: Halbedelsteine mit Golddraht
Entwurf Max Bill, SWB, Zürich

5 Schmucksachen
aus verschiedenen Materialien
in primitiver Technik ausgeführt
wobei der künstlerische Einfall für die Form
massgebend ist
Entwurf Harry Bertoia (USA)

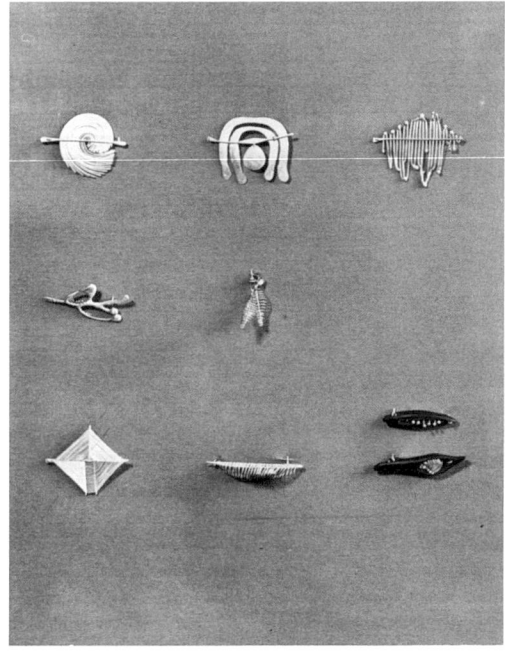

Halskette
aus vielen geschlungenen Kettchen
in Rosenquarz
einfache, lebendige Form
natürliche Materialwirkung

Jewelry

Three finger rings
left: from a single, unsoldered wire
right: three uniform plates
of different-colored gold
center: semiprecious stones with gold wire
Design: Max Bill, SWB, Zurich

Five pieces of jewelry
made of various materials
Executed using primitive techniques
with artistic ideas determining the form
Design: Harry Bertoia (USA)

Necklace
made of several intertwined chains
of rose quartz
Simple, lively form
Emphasis on the natural effect of the material

Schlechtwetterkleidung

Wetterhut
mit Ohrenschutz und Sturmband
elegante, einfache Form
Modell Jacob Scherrer AG. Romanshorn

Schlechtwetterbekleidung
Jupe, Jacke
Kappe mit Gesichtsschirm
und Haarschutz
Modell ‚Marquesa' Jacob Scherrer AG.
Romanshorn

Windjacke lose Form
praktischer Aermelverschluss
Modell Jacob Scherrer AG. Romanshorn

Rainwear

Rain hat
with ear flaps and chinstrap
Elegant, simple form
Model: Jacob Scherrer AG, Romanshorn

Rainwear
Skirt, jacket
Cap with visor
and hair protector
Model: Marquesa, by Jacob Scherrer AG,
Romanshorn

Loose-fitting windbreaker
Practical sleeve straps
Model: Jacob Scherrer AG, Romanshorn

Forms in various appliances and modes of transportation

Damenschuhe

Sandalette
in schöner formaler Durchbildung
besonders flexible Sohlen
Hersteller Bally AG. Schönenwerd
Verkauf Arola-Schuh AG. Zürich

Damen-Trotteur
der Grundform des Fusses angepasst
formal und technisch einwandfrei
Hersteller Bally AG. Schönenwerd
Verkauf Arola-Schuh AG. Zürich

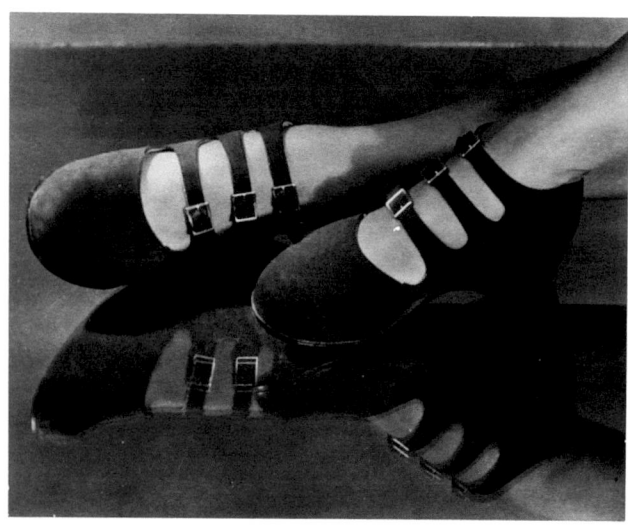

Strassenschuh
marineblau mit Keilabsatz
harmonische Form, dem Fuss angepasst
gute Stütze,
nach individueller Ristform verschliessbar
Schwedisches Modell ‚Hästen'

Women's Shoes

Sandals
with beautifully designed form
Especially flexible soles
Manufacturer: Bally AG, Schönenwerd
Sold by: Arola-Schuh AG, Zurich

Women's oxfords
adapted to basic shape of foot
Formally and technically ideal
Manufacturer: Bally AG, Schönenwerd
Sold by: Arola-Schuh AG, Zurich

Street shoes
Navy blue with wedge heel
Harmonious form, adapted to the foot
Good support, with adjustable straps to fit
individual instep
Swedish model Hästen

Herrenschuhe

Ski-Schuh
rationelle Lösung aus der Funktion
als Ausdruck der Skifahrtechnik
Modell Rominger - Bally AG. Schönenwerd
Verkauf Arola-Schuh AG. Zürich

Staub, Zürich

Winterschuh
Oberteil Schaffell
Unterteil bis zur Nässezone Leder
Hersteller Bally AG. Schönenwerd
Verkauf Arola-Schuh AG. Zürich

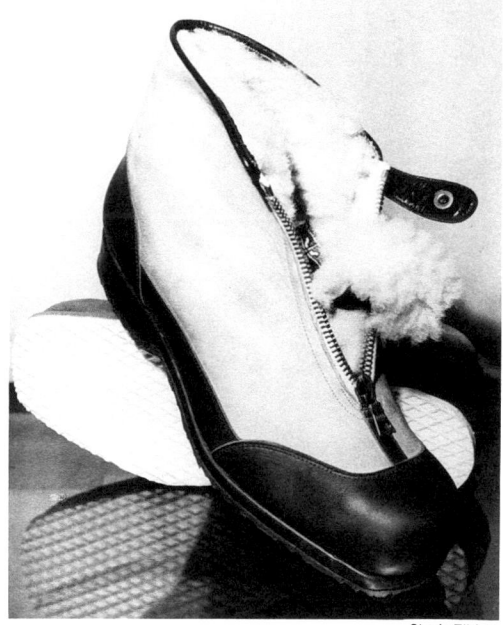

Staub, Zürich

Herren-Halbschuh
der Fussform angepasst
braunes Wildleder
Hersteller Bally AG. Schönenwerd
Verkauf Arola-Schuh AG. Zürich

Staub, Zürich

Men's Shoes

Ski shoe
Rational solution derived from function
as expression of skiing technique
Model: Rominger—Bally AG, Schönenwerd
Sold by: Arola-Schuh AG, Zurich

Winter shoe
Upper in sheepskin
Lower section down to wet zone in leather
Manufacturer: Bally AG, Schönenwerd
Sold by: Arola-Schuh AG, Zurich

Men's mid-height shoe
Adapted to shape of foot
Brown suede
Manufacturer: Bally AG, Schönenwerd
Sold by: Arola-Schuh AG, Zurich

Büro-Apparate

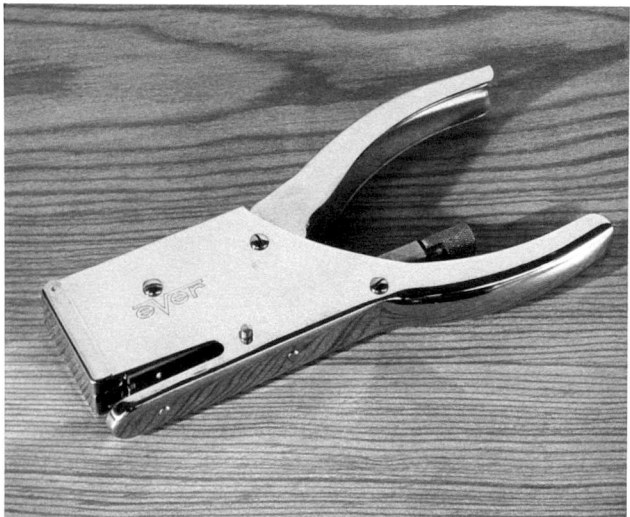

Heftzange
gepresstes Eisenblech, verchromt
einfache Formgebung
gute Firmenbezeichnung
Vertrieb Adolf Görlitz, Zürich

Heiniger, Zürich

Rechenmaschine
Eisenblechkarosserie mit Schrumpflack
einfache, klare Gestaltung aller Teile
gute Placierung der Firmenmarke
Hersteller Ing. C. Olivetti & Co. S.p.A. Ivrea-Turin

Heiniger, Zürich

Diktierapparat
einfache, übersichtliche Gestaltung
Hersteller Beka St. Aubin AG., St. Aubin
Vertrieb Steiner AG., Bern

Office Devices

Stapler
Pressed sheet iron, chrome-plated
Simple design
Good placement of company name
Sold by: Adolf Görlitz, Zurich

Calculating machine
Sheet-iron housing with wrinkle-finish paint
Simple, clear-cut design of all parts
Good placement of company logo
Manufacturer: engineers C. Olivetti & Co. S.p.A., Ivrea-Turin

Dictaphone
Simple, clearly arranged design
Manufacturer: Beka St. Aubin AG, St. Aubin
Sold by: Steiner AG, Bern

Schreibmaschinen

Reise-Schreibmaschine
besonders kleine und leichte Ausführung
kann einschliesslich Etui
in der Aktenmappe untergebracht werden
klare formale Durchbildung
Herstellung Paillard S.A., Yverdon
Vertrieb Hermag,
Hermes-Schreibmaschinen AG., Zürich

Heiniger, Zürich

Reise-Schreibmaschine
als kleine Büromaschine verwendbar
Versuch einer einfachen Durchgestaltung
des Gehäuses
Mitarbeiter für die Form Max Bill SWB, Zürich
Hersteller Aug. Birchmeier's Söhne, Murgenthal

Heiniger, Zürich

Büro-Schreibmaschine
sorgfältige konstruktive
und formale Durchbildung
Farbe graubeige
Formgebung Architekt Nizzoli, Milano
Hersteller Ing. C. Olivetti & Co. S.p.A. Ivrea-Turin

Heiniger, Zürich

Typewriters

Travel typewriter
Especially small and lightweight model
Fits with case into a briefcase
Clear, formal design
Manufacturer: Paillard S.A., Yverdon
Sold by: Hermag, Hermes-Schreibmaschinen AG, Zurich

Travel typewriter
Can be used as small office machine
Attempt at a simple but harmonious
housing design
Employees for the Form Max Bill, SWB, Zurich
Manufacturer: Aug. Birchmeier's Söhne, Murgenthal

Office typewriter
Carefully considered structural
and formal design
Color: gray-beige
Design: architect Nizzoli, Milan
Manufacturer: engineers C. Olivetti & Co. S.p.A., Ivrea-Turin

Forms in various appliances and modes of transportation

Autos

Cabriolet
Schweiz. Spezialkarosserie auf Rover-Chassis
sorgfältig ausgewogene Form
ohne Uebertreibung
zweckmässige Anordnung der verchromten
Schutzleisten
Hersteller Carosserie Graber, Wichtrach, Bern

Jeep, ein Vielzweckfahrzeug
Kleinlastwagen, Personenauto, Kleintraktor
4 unabhängig angetriebene Räder
robust und zweckmässig
bis zur Unverwüstlichkeit
Konstruktion Willis Knight

Heiniger, Zürich

Sportwagen
geschlossene Form weitgehend in Stromlinie
Maximalgeschwindigkeit 185 km/h
Carosserie Farina, Milano
Hersteller Cisitalia, Torino

Automobiles

Convertible
Special Swiss body on Rover chassis
Carefully balanced form
without exaggeration
Functional arrangement of chrome-plated
protective strips
Manufacturer: Carosserie Graber, Wichtrach, Bern

Jeep, a multipurpose vehicle
Small truck, passenger car, small tractor
Four-wheel drive
Robust and functional
to the point of indestructibility
Design: Willis Knight

Sports car
Largely streamlined, closed form
Maximum speed is 185 kmh
Body: Farina, Milan
Manufacturer: Cisitalia, Turin

Schienenauto

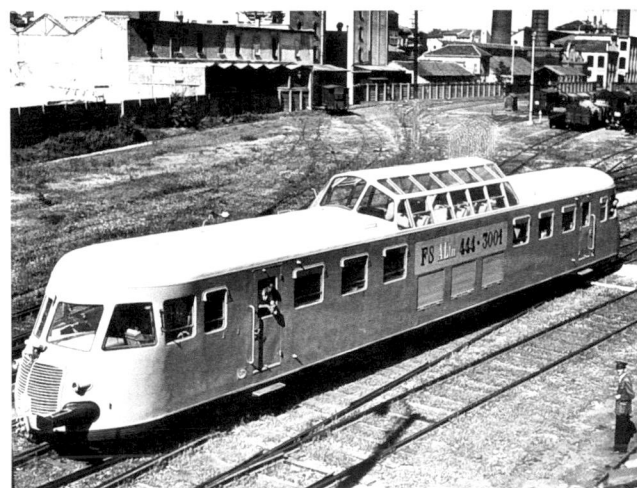

Schienenauto der italienischen Staatsbahnen
maximale Reisegeschwindigkeit
auf Hauptlinien 130 km/h
zentral gelegte Panorama-Kuppel
Gestaltung Architekt Renzo Zavanello, Milano
Hersteller O. M. Milano

Panorama-Kuppel im Schienenauto
bewegliche Rücklehnen der Bestuhlung
saubere konstruktive Durchbildung aller Teile
Gestaltung Architekt Renzo Zavanello, Milano
Hersteller O. M. Milano

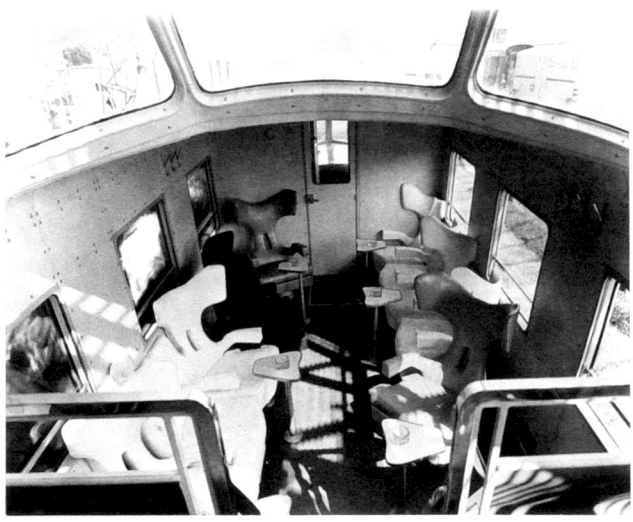

Gesellschaftsraum im Schienenauto
der italienischen Staatsbahnen
teilweise frei drehbare Fauteuils
in verschiedenfarbigem Leder
Betonung des Reisens als Vergnügen
Gestaltung Architekt Renzo Zavanello, Milano
Hersteller O. M. Milano

Rail Buses

Rail bus of the Italian State Railways
Maximum traveling speed on the main lines
is 130 kmh
Central panoramic dome
Design: architect Renzo Zavenello, Milan
Manufacturer: O. M., Milan

Panoramic dome in rail bus
Seats with movable backrests
Clean-lined structural design of all parts
Design: architect Renzo Zavenello, Milan
Manufacturer: O. M., Milan

Lounge in the rail bus
of the Italian State Railways
Armchairs, some of them swiveling,
in leather of various colors
Emphasis on travel as a pleasant pastime
Design: architect Renzo Zavenello, Milan
Manufacturer: O. M., Milan

Eisenbahnwagen

Personenwagen der Schweiz. Bundesbahnen
aus der Leichtschnellzugskomposition
sorgfältige formale und konstruktive
Durchbildung
Hersteller Schweiz. Wagons-
und Aufzügefabrik AG. Schlieren-Zürich

Personenwagen 3. Klasse
der Schweiz. Bundesbahnen
rationelle, solide, formal
und konstruktiv einwandfreie Lösung
Innengestaltung Arch. Gebr. Pfister, Zürich
Hersteller Schweiz. Wagons-
und Aufzügefabrik AG. Schlieren-Zürich

Speisewagen der Schweiz. Bundesbahnen
klare Gestaltung aller Teile
einheitliche Verwendung von Leichtmetall
Innengestaltung Arch. Gebr. Pfister, Zürich
Hersteller Schweiz. Wagons-
und Aufzügefabrik AG. Schlieren-Zürich

Train Cars

Swiss Federal Railways passenger car
from a lightweight express train
Carefully considered formal and structural design
Manufacturer: Schweiz. Wagons-
und Aufzügefabrik AG, Schlieren-Zurich

Swiss Federal Railways third-class passenger car
Rational, solid, formally and
structurally ideal solution
Interior design: architects Gebr. Pfister, Zurich
Manufacturer: Schweiz. Wagons-
und Aufzügefabrik AG, Schlieren-Zurich

Swiss Federal Railways dining car
Clear-lined design of all parts
Uniform use of light metal
Interior design: architects Gebr. Pfister, Zurich
Manufacturer: Schweiz. Wagons-
und Aufzügefabrik AG, Schlieren-Zurich

Triebwagen

Lokomotive d. Berner Alpenbahngesellschaft
Bern-Lötschberg-Simplon
Stundenleistung 4000 PS an der Motorwelle
Dienstgewicht 80 t, Spitzengeschwindigkeit
125 km h
Hersteller Brown Boveri & Co. AG. Baden
Aufbau Schweizerische Lokomotiv- und
Maschinenfabrik, Winterthur

Triebwagen der Aigle-Leysin-Bahn
mit 2 Brown Boveri Gleichstrommotoren
mit je 130 kW Stundenleistung
Fahrgeschwindigkeit 14 km h
sorgfältige Durchbildung der äusseren Form
Hersteller Brown Boveri & Co. AG. Baden
Aufbau Schweizerische Lokomotiv- und
Maschinenfabrik, Winterthur

Vierachsiger Leichttriebwagen
der Strassenbahn Zürich
Simplex-Drehgestell Typ Brown Boveri
Totalleistung der 4 Motoren 162 kW
maximale Fahrgeschwindigkeit 60 km h
Hersteller Brown Boveri & Co. AG. Baden
Aufbau Industriegesellschaft Neuhausen

Rail Cars

Locomotive of the Bern Alpine Railway
Bern-Lötschberg-Simplon
Hourly capacity of 4,000 hp(M) at the engine shaft
Service weight is 80 t, top speed is 125 kmh
Manufacturer: Brown Boveri & Co. AG, Baden
Superstructure: Schweizerische Lokomotiv- und
Maschinenfabrik, Winterthur

Rail car of the Aigle-Leysin Railway
with two Brown Boveri direct-current motors,
each providing 130 kW hourly capacity
Traveling speed is 14 kmh
Carefully considered design of the outer form
Manufacturer: Brown Boveri & Co. AG, Baden
Superstructure: Schweizerische Lokomotiv- und
Maschinenfabrik, Winterthur

Four-axle light-rail car
used in the Zurich tram system
Simplex pivoted bogie of the Brown Boveri type
Total capacity of the four engines is 162 kW
Maximum traveling speed 60 kmh
Manufacturer: Brown Boveri & Co. AG, Baden
Superstructure: Industriegesellschaft Neuhausen

Forms in various appliances and modes of transportation

Flugzeuge

Düsenflugzeug
absolute Zweckform
aus den Bedürfnissen entwickelt
britische Konstruktion, Typ Fairchild

Schwanzloses Flugzeug
neuartige Gestaltung
eines Konstruktionsproblems
das schon gelöst schien
Konstruktion Armstrong Whitworth

K.L.M. News Service, Zürich

Passagier-Transportflugzeug
Typ ‚Konstellation'
aerodynamische Durchbildung bis ins Letzte
ergibt eine selbstverständliche Form
gleich Formen in der Natur

Airplanes

Jet
Absolutely functional form
developed from the needs at hand
British design, Fairchild type

Tailless plane
Novel design to solve
a structural problem
that seemed to already be resolved
Design: Armstrong Whitworth

Passenger airplane
Constellation type
Aerodynamic design down to the last detail
results in a matter-of-fact form
resembling forms in nature

Forms in various appliances and modes of transportation

Ton-Uebertragung

Telefon-Tischstation
sinnvolle und praktische Anordnung aller Teile
Saubere konstruktive Durchführung
Hersteller Hasler AG. Bern

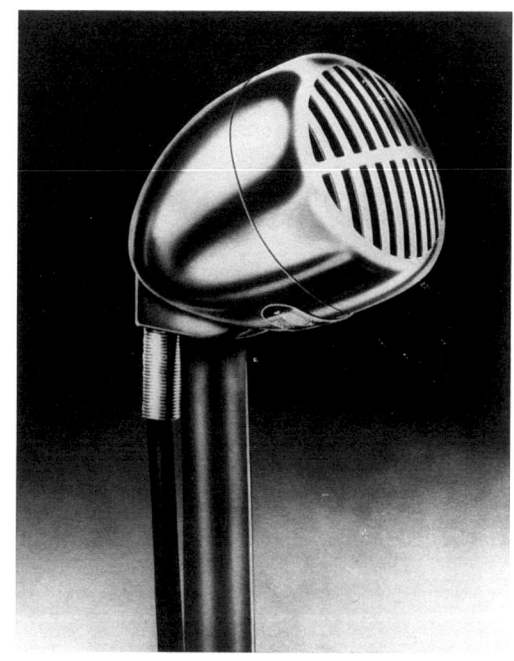

Mikrophon
saubere Gestaltung
bei minimalem Materialaufwand
Hersteller Shure Brothers, Chicago
Generalvertretung Telion AG. Zürich

Telefonhörer
mit eingebauter Wählscheibe
Einfache, praktische Konstruktion
bei schöner, formaler Durchbildung
Studienmodell von R. Lysell
für L.-M. Ericsson, Stockholm

Audio Transmission

Tabletop telephone station
Sensible and practical arrangement of all parts
Clean-lined structural execution
Manufacturer: Hasler AG, Bern

Microphone
Clean-lined design, with minimal use
of materials
Manufacturer: Shure Brothers, Chicago
General sales agency: Telion AG, Zurich

Telephone receiver
with built-in dial
Simple, practical structure
with a pleasing, formal design
Study model by R. Lysell
for L.-M. Ericsson, Stockholm

Bild-Uebermittlung

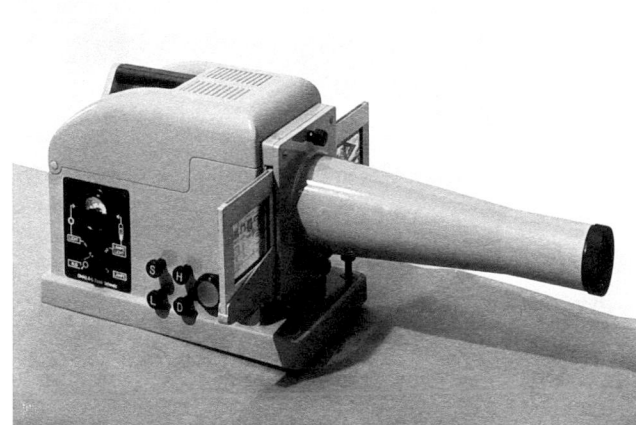

Projektionsapparat
einheitliche Durchbildung aller Elemente
Helles Gehäuse, Bedienungsteile schwarz
Modell Ing. Leo Wyrsch, Zürich
Hersteller OMAG Optik & Mechanik AG.
Basel-Neuallschwil

Empfangsstation für Television
Heimempfänger in formschöner
zweckmässiger Ausführung
Studienmodell von Derek Rabley

Universal Foto-Kamera „Hilba"
umfassende Anwendungsmöglichkeiten
Aeusserste Zweckmässigkeit der Konstruktion
ergibt die Formschönheit des Modells
Hersteller Hilfiker, Baumann & Co., Zürich

Image Transmission

Projection device
Harmonious design of all elements
Light-colored housing, black operating parts
Model: engineer Leo Wyrsch, Zurich
Manufacturer: OMAG Optik & Mechanik AG,
Basel-Neuallschwil

Receiver station for television
Home receiver in formally pleasing and
functional design
Study model by Derek Rabley

Hilba universal photo camera
Wide range of uses
Extreme functionality of design
results in the formal beauty of the model
Manufacturer: Hilfiker, Baumann & Co., Zurich

Forms in various appliances and modes of transportation

Radio-Empfangsapparate

Klein-Radio
technisch einwandfreie und zugleich
formschöne Gestaltung
Modell Eden Minns
Hersteller Murphy Radio Ltd.

Radioempfänger für Reise und Heim
konstruktiv und formal sorgfältig durchdacht
Robuste Ausführung
Vermeidung jeder überflüssigen Zutat
Modell Ing. Niklaus Eltz, Wien
Hersteller Radione AG. Wien
schweiz. Generalvertretung Max Funk, Zürich

Heim-Empfänger
durch neuartige Anordnung der Bestandteile
ist der traditionelle Kasten vermieden
Dadurch entsteht ein ansprechender Apparat
Amerikanisches Studienmodell

Radio Receivers

Small radio
Technically ideal design
combined with a pleasing form
Model: Eden Minns
Manufacturer: Murphy Radio Ltd.

Radio receiver for travel and home
Carefully considered structural and formal design
Robust execution
Avoidance of all superfluous elements
Model: engineer Niklaus Eltz, Vienna
Manufacturer: Radione AG, Vienna
Swiss sales agency: Max Funk, Zurich

Home receiver
Avoidance of traditional box
through novel arrangement of components
This creates an attractive device
American study model

Wohnräume

Wohnraum
in californischem Landhaus
direkte Verbindung mit dem Garten
ganze Wand als Schiebefenster
Architekt Richard J. Neutra, Los Angeles

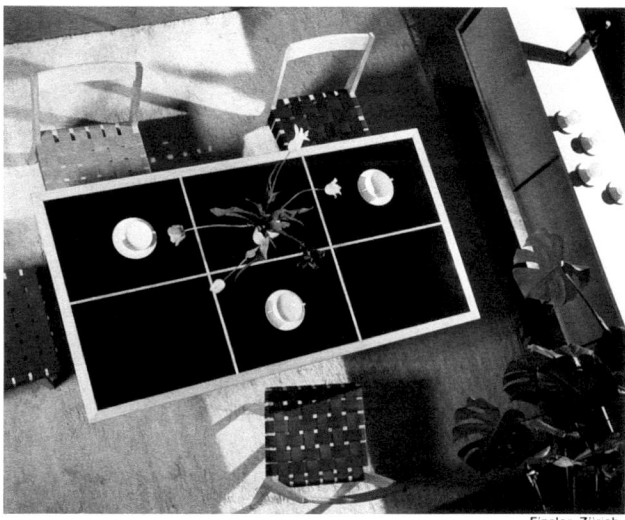

Wohnraum
mit Serienmöbeln
verschiedener Herkunft
Einrichtung mit Wohnbedarf-Typen

Möblierung eines Siedlungshauses
mit Serienmöbeln
verschiedener Herkunft
Einrichtung Architekten Cramer, Jaray,
Paillard, Zürich

Living Rooms

Living room
in California country home
Direct access to the garden
Entire wall as sliding glass door
Architect: Richard J. Neutra, Los Angeles

Living room
with mass-produced furniture
of various origins
Furnishing a room with standard elements

Furnishing a home in a housing development
with mass-produced furniture
of various origins
Interior decoration: architects Cramer, Jaray,
Paillard, Zurich

die gute form—good design also as a configuration of panels
jakob bill

the decision by the swiss werkbund (swb) to commission max bill to create the exhibition *die gute form* can be traced back to the success with which bill had already drawn attention to design criteria through his various activities and interventions.[1] since these latter were not confined simply to a small group of appliances or buildings, a host of themes occurred to him, which he represented with the aid of individual panels and organized into a sequence. to our great good fortune, these panels still survive in good condition even after more than 60 years.

every meaningful sequence presupposes a selective, ordering process. this is also the case with the panels of the exhibition *die gute form.* many of the panels today carry two numbers on the back. what do these figures signify? what purpose did they serve, and when? the first number—looking almost as if printed, but probably executed in black ink—appears to date from the same period as the panels themselves[2] and is today used as the inventory number. the second—handwritten and facing different directions— follows a different order. can a correlation be established between these two sets of numbers or can they be linked with other facts?

after receiving the commission from the swb,[3] max bill—based in his office in jenatschstrasse in zurich's enge district—worked on the content and design of the exhibition. he thereby conceived not only the mobile panels and their specially designed supports, but also their organization according to themes. he also finalized the selection and grouping of the products that were to be displayed as actual objects, and designed the entrance area and the publications relating to the exhibition. bill thus took charge of all aspects of the exhibition, ranging from the choice of examples of "good design" and their theoretical justification all the way to the architecture and presentation. at the first stop in basel, he also showed one of his own sculptures in the entrance area: *rhythm in space* (p. 5). max bill published a tall and narrow 16-page illustrated booklet to accompany the exhibition. it featured exclusively swiss products that matched his criteria of "good design," including two objects designed by himself. a photograph of his sculpture *continuity* (1946/47, destroyed 1948)—chosen probably not without self-interest—adorns the front cover. and lastly, on the day of the opening bill stood at the entrance to the exhibition and personally handed out these booklets to the public (pp. 36/37).

to return to the two sets of numbers mentioned above: since the exhibition was scheduled to travel to a number of different locations in switzerland and abroad following its first presentation at the mustermesse basel trade fair (may 7–17, 1949), the panels were produced in duplicate. one set

1 max bill joined the swb in 1930. his earliest writings on the design of items of everyday use date from the 1940s. see jakob bill (ed.), *max bill, funktion und funktionalismus—schriften: 1945–1988* (bern/sulgen, 2008). bill discusses the subject of exhibition design in the article "ausstellungen," in *Werk* 3 (1948), pp. 65–69.

2 according to renate menzi, head of the design collection at zurich's museum für gestaltung, all the panels already carried these numbers, which appear on round labels, when they entered the collection: "as perfect as if stencilled," thus Menzi.

3 no commission in writing from the swb has yet come to light. max bill's estimate of the total costs of the exhibition dates from Feb. 9, 1949. in a letter of Feb. 21, 1949 he enquires: "please let me know how much progress has been made in bern regarding the approval of the credit, so that i can make a start on the actual work for the exhibition *die gute form*." (document in the max, binia + jakob bill foundation, adligenswil)

was destined for switzerland ("die gute form S"), the other for germany ("die gute form D") (p. 151). the first set toured switzerland, austria, and the netherlands from may 1949 to may 1951, while the second was shown between may 1949 and june 1950, partly in conjunction with the *neues wohnen* exhibition organized by the german werkbund. some venues evidently put themselves forward for inclusion in the circuit (ulm, darmstadt). no layout plans exist for any of the shows in germany and it would appear from the correspondence that, for financial reasons, they were not requested. for the majority of venues visited by the version, by contrast, we have ground plans and lists of panels by max bill. he thus had full design responsibility only for the presentation of the swiss version "die gute form S", under the patronage of the swb and the pro helvetia federal cultural foundation. the ground plan of the layout in basel and other venues was regularly reproduced in schematic form in later publications.[4] the individual panels are thereby not numbered, but simply grouped into sections by theme.

since the show was conceived as a traveling exhibition, it had to be adaptable to the various rooms and spaces in which it was staged. max bill therefore designed a stand system consisting of individual modules that could be connected together (pp. 33–35). additional stability was provided by wire stays anchored to the walls. this system allowed complete flexibility when it came to the order of the panels, albeit with the one stipulation that the basic form—not least for static reasons—had to be curved. this is apparent from the ground plans designed for the various exhibition venues. as we shall see below, such serpentine forms are no exception in max bill's visual vocabulary. with the design of the curving lines, he simultaneously lent expression to what he himself defined as "good design."

the individual frames, labeled *gestelle* (stands) on the plan, were 48 cm wide and 3 m tall and were constructed with the simplest means from roof battens and a crosspiece (p. 140). the display panels were affixed to the stands by means of screws ending in right-angle hooks. Since the panels had to be mounted several times during the tour and by different people each time, there was a danger that they would suffer damage at the point at which they rested on the screws. To prevent this, metal shells were mounted on the panels at the corresponding four points, where they appear as semicircular discs: a simple but effective protection and support solution that was compelling at both the functional and the aesthetic level.

among the archival sources relating to the layout in basel is a list of panels with subject titles and numbers. it is immediately apparent that this original numbering does not correspond to that by which the panels are

[4] most recently in karin gimmi (ed.), *max bill—arquitecto/architect. 2G—revista internacional de arquitectura,* 29/30 (2004), pp. 98–101.

identified today (p. 150). for a reconstruction of the exhibition, however, we are nevertheless obliged to start from the latter system, since it represents the first reference numbers we have. the max bill archive[5] also houses a plan drawn by bill himself, in which he has sketched in the basic, rectangular structure of the basel exhibition space (pp. 134/35). the entire exhibition is laid out on top of this basic grid, which reproduces the divisions of the ceiling. the numbered panels are arranged in a curving constellation in the center of the hall, while the product exhibits are distributed on rectangular plinths along the walls. both display structures take account of the above-mentioned basic grid, whereby the angular and round forms harmonize with and mutually accentuate each other.

upon entering the exhibition hall, the visitor was greeted by a concave arrangement of five panels on which a red arrow indicated the direction of travel. the actual exhibition began on the sixth panel, which now changed angle to become the start of a convex bay. the first section was devoted to *formen der natur, wissenschaft, kunst, technik* ("forms in nature, science, art and technology") and ended with panel 20. panel 21 formed the back of panel 20 and led into a deeper, more enclosed bay that presented *formen der planung und architektur* ("forms in planning and architecture"), which continued up to and including panel 40. from here the display continued on the reverse of the stands, following a correspondingly convex line, with a section devoted to *formen des wohnbedarfs* ("forms in home fittings and furnishings"; panels 41–63). the transition from items of furniture to household appliances was marked by the change of angle from convex to concave. The fourth and final section of the exhibition, *formen verschiedener geräte und der verkehrstechnik* ("forms in various appliances and modes of transport"; panels 64–80), occupied the organically concave bay leading back to the hall entrance. it is immediately apparent that the switch between concave and convex in each case marked the transition from one subject area to the next. there is also a plan showing what is described— in max bill's own hand—as a "longitudinal section" (*längsschnitt*) of topics I and II (pp. 134/35). the plans for the frame-and-panel construction and for the front entrance were done by one of bill's assistants.

after basel, the next stops made by *die gute form* in 1949 in switzerland are sadly barely documented. bill's plan for the presentation in the gewerbemuseum bern (september 24–october 16, 1949)[6] appears to have been lost during the museum's later restructuring and no list of panels is known. at the swiss radio exhibition in zurich (august 25–30, 1949), only a reduced number of panels were shown (again, no corresponding list survives). we do at least have two photos of the show (p. 151), plus a short press release.

5 the max bill archive is held by the max, binia + jakob bill foundation, adligenswil.

6 the bern gewerbemuseum no longer exists in its previous form and is today the kornhausforum.

how the second set of panels was numbered, we do not know. this german version made its first stop in cologne, where it was included in the werkbund's *neues wohnen* exhibition (may 14–july 3, 1949), which thus opened at almost exactly the same time as the basel mustermesse; its presentation there is not documented.[7] the exhibition next moved on to the council chamber in constance town hall (august 13–29, 1949). the chamber's solid wooden furnishings meant that the stands could not be used, and so the panels were suspended from the ceiling (middle row p. 151). max bill attended the opening and wrote to the then quaestor of the swb, berchtold von grünigen: "on saturday i was in constance, where *die gute form* is on show in the council chamber. the whole of constance is decked with flags, with banners for *die gute form* strung between them" (middle row, left p. 151). the town has made a great effort in this respect. ulm has promised me something 'at least just as attractive.' the speeches by the mayor of constance, the french military governor, and the architect blomeier, chairman of the south baden werkbund, were very gratifying. the swiss consulate was also represented. the show was well received and attendance in the afternoon was likewise good. best of all, however, was the drinks reception in the spitalkeller later on, attended by a small group, with a delicious gourmet meal."[8]

the show's next stop, in the municipal museum in ulm (october 9–30, 1949), was organized by inge scholl, at that time head of the ulm volkshochschule. max bill was not present at the vernissage on october 8, 1949, but wrote that same day to hans finsler, chairman of the swb, that the city of darmstadt wanted to host *die gute form* together with another swiss traveling exhibition, *deine wohnung – dein nachbar – deine heimat (your apartment—your neighbor—your home)*. after ulm, *die gute form* was supposed to have been shown in the landesgewerbemuseum in stuttgart; in the end, however, it was simply temporarily stored there.

the presentation in darmstadt (december 16, 1949–start of 1950) is documented in a sketch by the architect and designer c.w. voltz, a "student" of max bill. the layout was rectilinear, with the panels displayed on top of the heater cladding along the walls. the second, separate exhibition was shown on screens arranged one behind the other down the middle of the room. max bill did not travel to this vernissage either, but "as the designer of one of the exhibitions" sent his apologies for december 16, 1949.[9] c.w. voltz described the resulting impression in a letter of december 21, 1949 as follows: "the illustrated panels were mounted and arranged in a wholly inept manner, with no coherence whatsoever in a cramped room. the result: experts and amateurs went away disappointed."

7 it is evident, however, that max bill sent the plan of the basel layout to the german werkbund, whose reply of Apr. 14, 1949 states: "as we have already informed you, we shall by and large keep the curve of your sketch for the exhibition, since it tallies completely with our own concept of an exhibition arrangement, and would therefore also like to make the roof-batten frames identical to your own." on May 9, 1949 max bill wrote: "i am enclosing the definitive plan for the exhibition and with it a list of the panels in order of hanging. i hope everything is clear." sadly neither the plan nor the accompanying list has survived.

8 letter of Aug. 17, 1949.

9 according to the timetable (p. 151, bottom row left), the exhibition was scheduled to open on Dec. 10, 1949. max bill's letter of Dec. 14, 1949. to darmstadt city council names Dec. 16 as the start date.

die gute form is known to have made two further stops, in kassel (march 25–april 23, 1950) and wuppertal (may 20–june 11, 1950), but details even as to precisely where the exhibition was housed are in both cases lacking. it is impossible to establish what subsequently became of the panels of the german version.

the swiss version that started out from basel is much better documented overall. lists and ground plans exist for most of the venues visited by the exhibition in austria and the netherlands. the list made by max bill on january 20, 1950, in the run-up to the exhibition at the akademie der bildenden künste in vienna, served as the reference from that point on. it takes up—with a few deviations—the original four sections (p. 150): panels 1–7 correspond to the section *formen der natur, wissenschaft, kunst, technik,* panels 8–24 to *formen der planung and architektur,* panels 25–60 to *formen verschiedener geräte und der verkehrsmittel* and panels 61–79 to *formen des wohnbedarfs.* (a maximum 79 of the altogether 80 panels were only ever shown in subsequent exhibitions, too.)

the numbering of the panels on the list of january 20, 1950 is identical to that found on the panels at the zurich hochschule der künste and today used as their inventory numbers. these neatly drawn numbers were probably added to the back of the panels at this point in time. since the layout of the exhibition had to be adapted to each new location, the order of the panels was never exactly the same. the numberings in vienna, linz, and graz, although broadly similar, were nevertheless different and were in each case recorded by hand alongside the original list.

at the akademie der bildenden künste in vienna (18 february–10 march 1950), the exhibition was held in two adjoining long and narrow galleries with windows alongside one side (pp. 136/37). this inspired max bill to draw a line from the entrance that snaked its way ever deeper into the room and ended at the last window. the numbers written on the plan correlate with the list of january 20, 1950. in total, 68 panels were included in the exhibition.

the plan for the landesmuseum in linz (march 25–mid-april 1950) shows the panels laid out in the shape of an "s" (p. 138);[10] they had to be accommodated in a very small room. the panels are numbered on the plan in an uninterrupted sequence from 1 to 68. this numbering was correlated with the reference list (20-1-50/vienna) accompanying the sketch. drawn by max bill himself, this is the only plan to show the position of the wire stays, which served to stabilize the stands.

10 the exhibition was hosted by the upper austrian werkbund, which had its headquarters in the landesmuseum in linz.

for the assembly hall of the technische hochschule in graz (april 20–
may 7, 1950), the panels were divided into three groups, concealed the
architecture of the end walls behind an undulating line and extended out in
the shape of a teardrop from between two windows into the center of the
room. the first ten panels appeared in the same order as in vienna, while
the remaining 57 followed a different sequence. on the plan, which carries
the signature of max bill, the panels are again numbered as per the list
of january 20, 1950 (p. 139).

the next exhibition, which took place in the kunstgewerbemuseum in zurich
(june 3– august 20, 1950) was completely different again to the previous
ones, in terms of both individual sequences and overall layout. sadly, no
definitive plan is preserved in the archive, but the accompanying list is
divided into ten sections of six panels each, with the exception of sections
VII and IX, which have twelve. this means that 72 panels were displayed.
it looks very much as if the exhibition was switched at short notice to a
different part of the museum. a sheet preserved in the archive shows a plan
of the main level, on top of which a layout similar to that used at the basel
mustermesse has been sketched. in the end, however, the exhibition was
staged in the gallery and hence had to be completely rethought. this
may well explain the eight sections of just six panels each. the two long
sequences were probably erected back to back. a visitor's guide was
published to accompany the exhibition and contained a foreword by director
johannes itten, the illustrations from the basel booklet plus a few more, and
a version of bill's text revised by the author.[11]

there still remains the second set of numbers, written by hand on the
back of the panels. these correspond to the order of display in the stedelijk
museum in amsterdam (february 18–march 10, 1950), with altogether
73 panels on the list, without the number 1, which was not awarded. on the
introduction panel (zhdk inv no 80), a 0 is written instead. it is likely that
this panel was eliminated in amsterdam prior to the final installation without
being replaced and correspondingly was not given a number; this would
bring the total number of panels back down to 72. on the original plan (drawn
by one of max bill's assistants), by contrast, panel 80 is shown on its own
in the antechamber outside the first of the five interconnecting galleries.
the numbering on the plan again follows the list of january 20, 1950, although
on the list relating to the actual exhibition, these numbers are given in
brackets and a continuous numbering is otherwise used. the question therefore arises as to when the second set of handwritten numbers was added
to the panels. this probably took place in amsterdam. here, too, moreover,
the panels—in a fashion not dissimilar to vienna—were laid out in concave

11 *die gute form*. no. 183 in the series of exhibition guides issued by the zurich kunstgewerbe-museum (undated but undoubtedly published to coincide with the exhibition in 1950). text without illustrations. see jakob bill, as note 1, pp. 27–30. printed here p. 146 f.

bays running from doorway to doorway, always opposite the windows (p. 136/37). the list is correspondingly divided into a group of panels introducing the main themesand subsequently divided in four sections.

it has not been possible to locate any documents relating to the exhibition's two other venues in the netherlands, the van abbemuseum in eindhoven (april 7–30, 1951) and the boymans van beuningen museum in rotterdam (may 5–end of may 1951).

max bill was so busy as an architect with the burgeoning plans for the hochschule für gestaltung in ulm, the competition for the swiss pavilion at the venice biennale, the design of the swiss pavilion at the milan triennale, and numerous lectures, that looking after the exhibition somewhat receded into the background. he was also involved in the preparation of a book based on the exhibition and exploring its ideas in greater depth, which was published in 1952 under the title *form—eine bilanz über die formentwicklung um die mitte des XX. jahrhunderts / form—a balance sheet of mid-twentieth-century trends in design.*

at the initiative of architect august boyer, plans were also made to present *die gute form* at the lucerne kunstmuseum in december 1950 (parallel to the christmas exhibition). in the end, however, this was too short notice and lucerne was therefore scheduled for june 1951, after the shows in the netherlands. this project never materialized, however.

despite certain objections leveled against it, the exhibition left a notable and enduring mark, most especially with the introduction in 1952 of the prize of the same name, "die gute form" (in french, "forme utile"). products that received this commendation were allowed to feature a round label specially designed for this purpose. in 1957 max bill published a small booklet about this "good design" prize with definitions and a number of illustrations.[12]

with regard to the panels chosen for display, it should be noted that the panel described as a "selection of swiss goods" (*schweizer warenkatalog,* zhdk inv. no. 81), which did not follow the general overall concept, was apparently never used on the exhibition tour. the panels featuring "flow forms," "train cars," "handles," "combination tables," and "rainwear" (*strömungsformen, schienenauto, handgriffe, kombinationstische* and *schlechtwetterkleidung* respectively), as well as the blank panels, were only shown in basel. by contrast, the panels "audio transmission," "image transmission," "radio receivers," and "living rooms" (*tonübertragung,*

12 max bill, *die gute form—6 jahre auszeichnung «die gute form»,* winterthur, 1957. in order to underline the continuity of the notion of "good design", max bill used the identical typeface to the booklet accompanying the first exhibition of *die gute form* at the 1949 basel mustermesse. here, too, he included two of his own product designs among the illustrations. see also the remarks on the prize "die gute form", which has nothing to do with the exhibition, in the text by claude lichtenstein, p. 26ff.

bildübermittlung, radioempfangsapparate and *wohnräume*) were only added after basel and surface for the first time on the list for vienna.[13] in austria the number of panels was further trimmed. in the kunstgewerbemuseum in zurich, by contrast, there was ample space to show a larger number.

as already mentioned, all the plan drawings by max bill visualize the rows of panels laid out in organically curving lines, independent of the orthogonal canon. the design itself was determined by the dimensions of the space in question, whereby the walls were not used as display surfaces. some readers may wonder whether these curving free-hand forms are at all compatible with the concrete aesthetic represented by max bill. they were: it should be remembered that, in the painting *three colors of equal length* (1946/47; p. 156), the lines placed seemingly freely in the pictorial plane are "mounted" within a dividing grid that is oriented both orthogonally and diagonally—a scheme that goes back to lively discussions between bill and his artist friend georges vantongerloo.[14] coming even closer to the ground plan for the exhibition are a small group of pictures, in particular those dating from 1947, in which mutually contrasting colors that unravel in space or towards their outer edges meet along a line. by way of example, we may mention here the works *unlimited and limited* (p. 157) and *emphasis of a spiral* (both 1947). where the centres of color lie in these paintings is where the panels stand in the exhibition. the panels for their part "broadcast" a message into the room that coalesces, as it were, with those of the neighboring panels, and the same thing happens in principle in these paintings. the double-looped band in *continuity* (1946/47) also exhibits convex and concave arcs. here, once again, two strands of activity from my father's life weave themselves together: on the one hand, his artistic work, and on the other, the exhibition architecture. this affinity naturally already exists in the first presentation of the exhibition *die gute form* in basel, at the entrance to which—to a certain extent as a frontispiece and leitmotif—he placed the plaster version of his sculpture *rhythm in space* (1947/48). that max bill, as a theoretician and an exhibition designer, should everywhere include examples of his own work is programmatic. it shows him taking the lead in all respects and is testimony that good design can also manifest itself as an exhibition and a configuration of panels.

13 this also falls in line with the press release that max bill wrote for the 1949 swiss radio exhibition in zurich: "the exhibition itself [...] is to be continuously expanded with new and better examples." nowhere is it stated, however, that panels were added to the german version. the swiss version was probably only updated for its tour to austria.

14 jakob bill, "vantongerloo—bill: comment l'aîné a influencé le cadet," in *georges vantongerloo 1886–1965: un pionnier de la sculpture moderne*, exh. cat. musée départemental matisse du cateau-cambrésis, paris (2007), pp. 176–83.

Jakob Bill was born in 1942 in Zurich as the son of Max and Binia Bill. He is an artist. Since 1957 his works have been shown in numerous solo and group exhibitions at home and abroad. From 1963 to 1971 Jakob Bill studied prehistory, classical archaeology, and art history at Zurich University and the Institute of Archaeology at London University (1964). In 1969 and 1972 he was awarded a Swiss federal art scholarship, and in 1971 gained his doctorate in prehistory. From 1972 to 1982 Jakob Bill worked as a research assistant at the Swiss National Museum in Zurich, and from 1982 to 1985 was the head of archaeological research in the Principality of Liechtenstein. In 1985 he was appointed the first full-time Lucerne cantonal archaeologist. Since 1996 Jakob Bill has been president of the max, binia + jakob bill foundation. He lives in Adligenswil (Lucerne) and Pianezzo (Ticino).

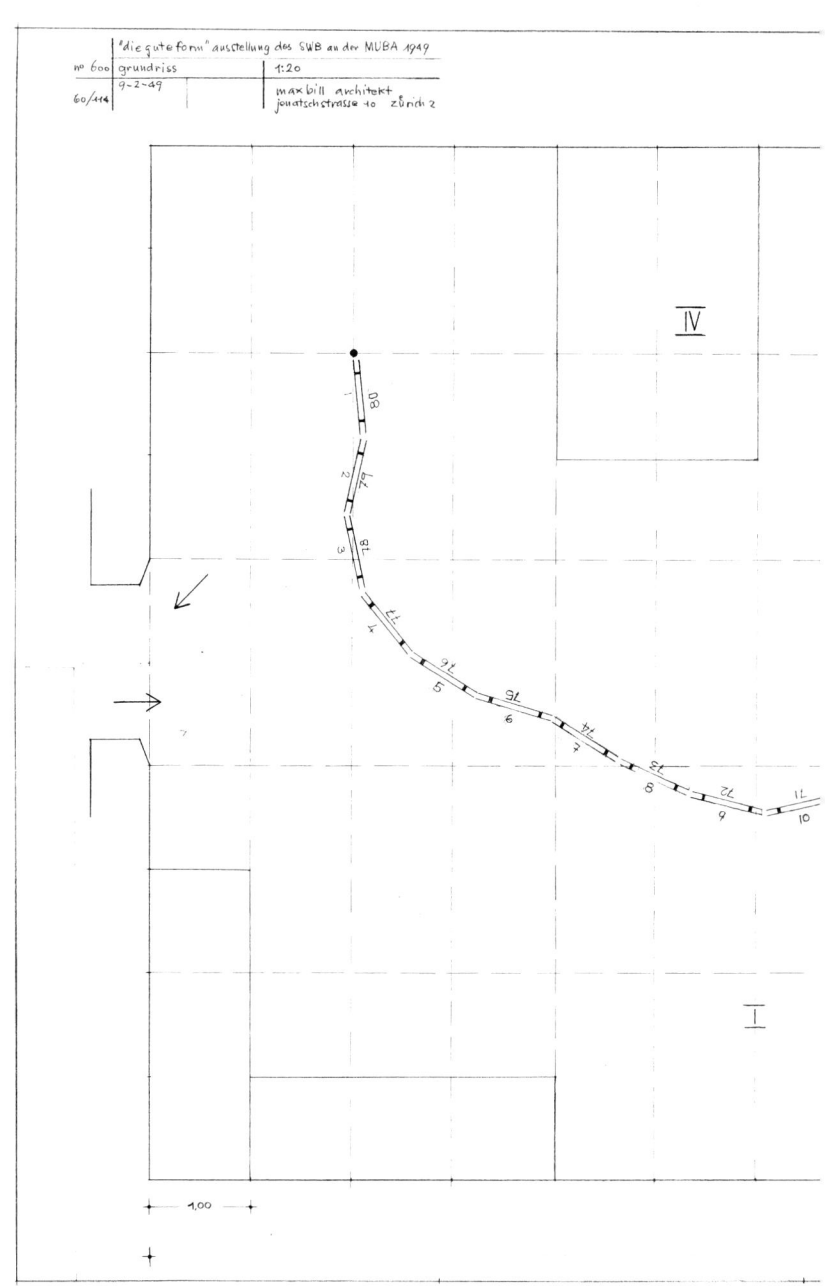

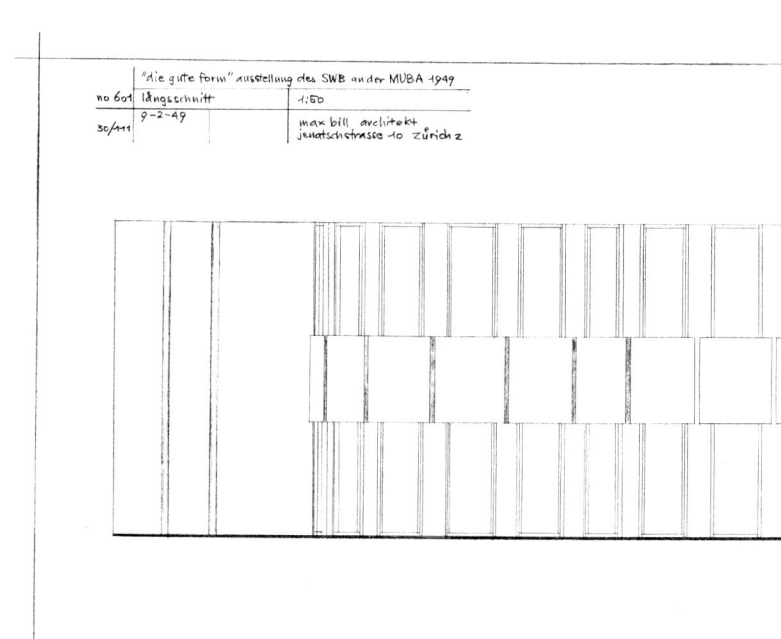

< The exhibition installation in Basel, probably shortly before the opening on May 7, 1949.

Max Bill: ground plan and elevation of the exhibition installation in Basel, as presented in May 1949. Visible on the ground plan is the square grid into which the curves of the panel layout are inscribed. The entrance to the show is on the left. The position and number of display plinths was modified in the course of the exhibition.

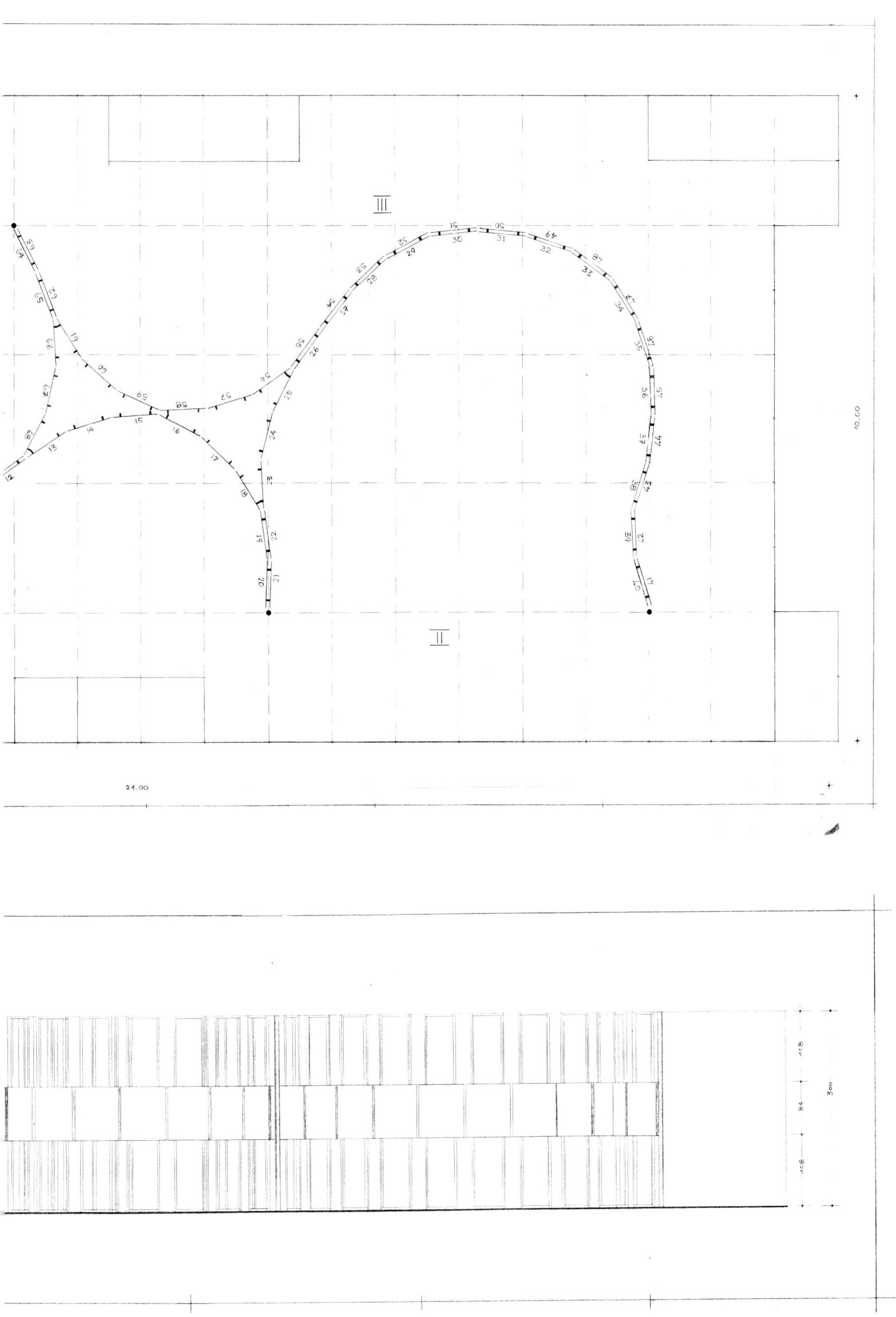

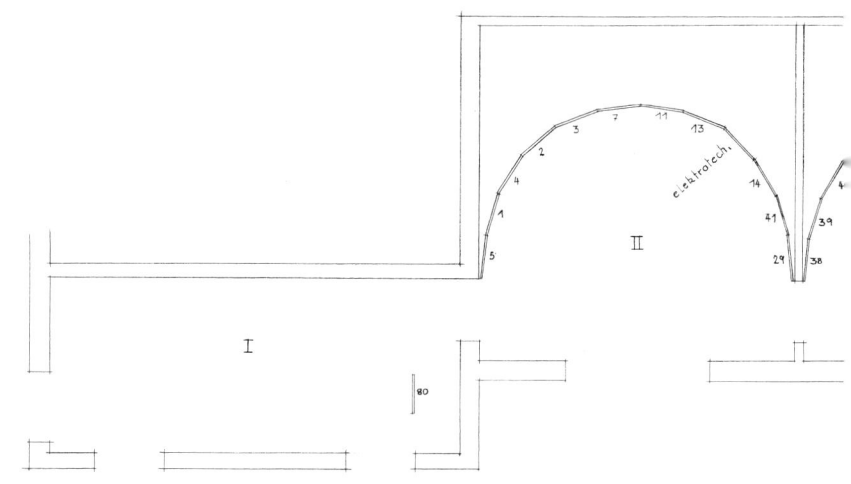

Ground plan of the exhibition in Amsterdam, 1951.

Situation at the Vienna exhibition venue, 1950.

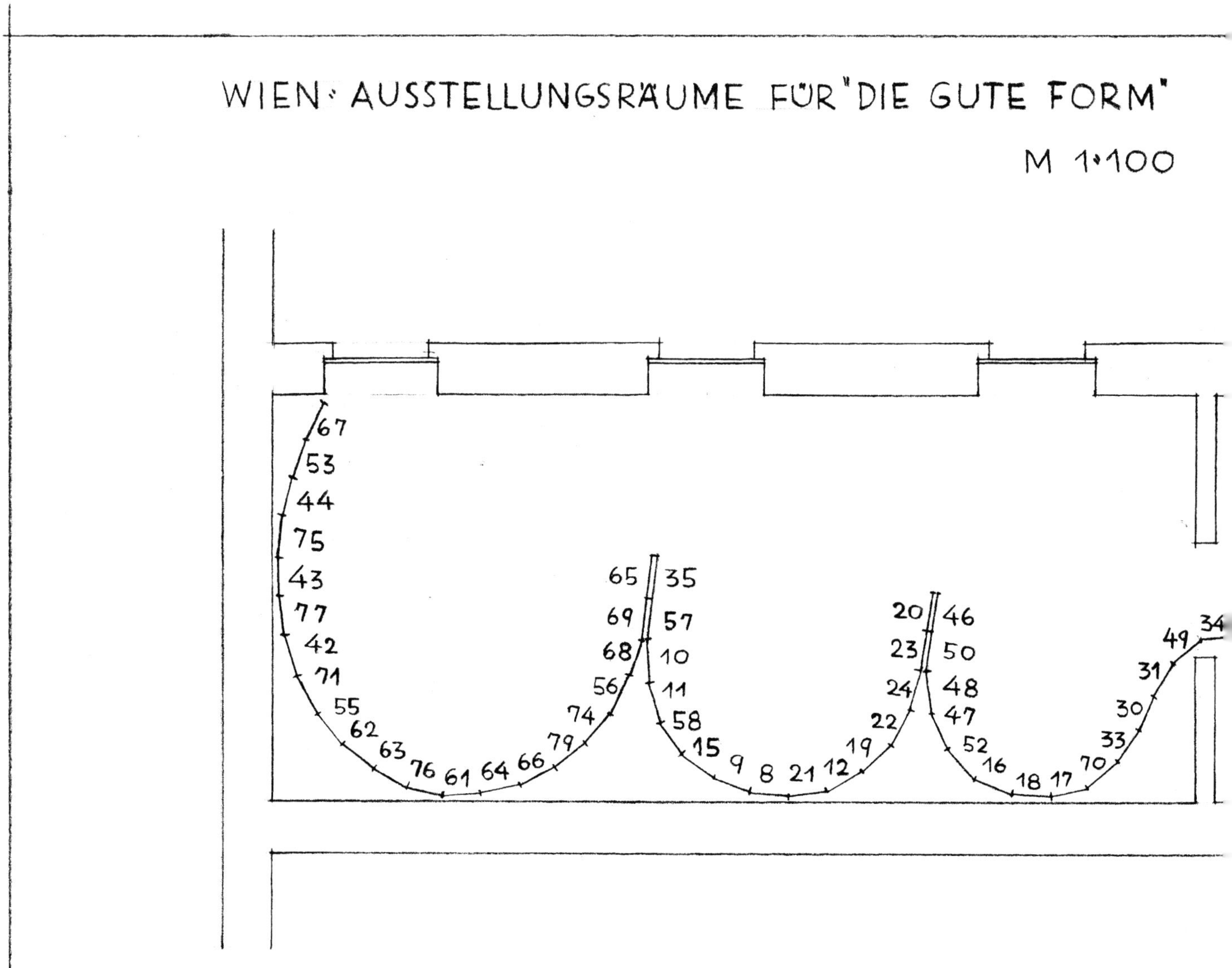

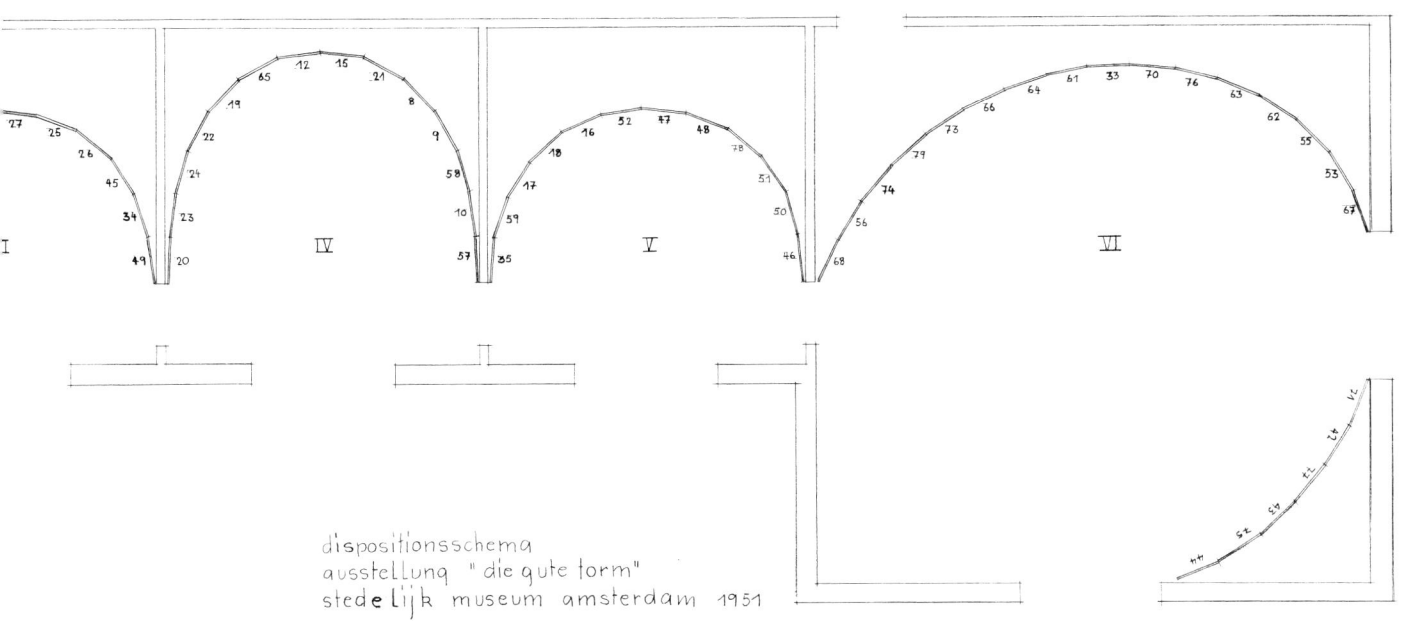

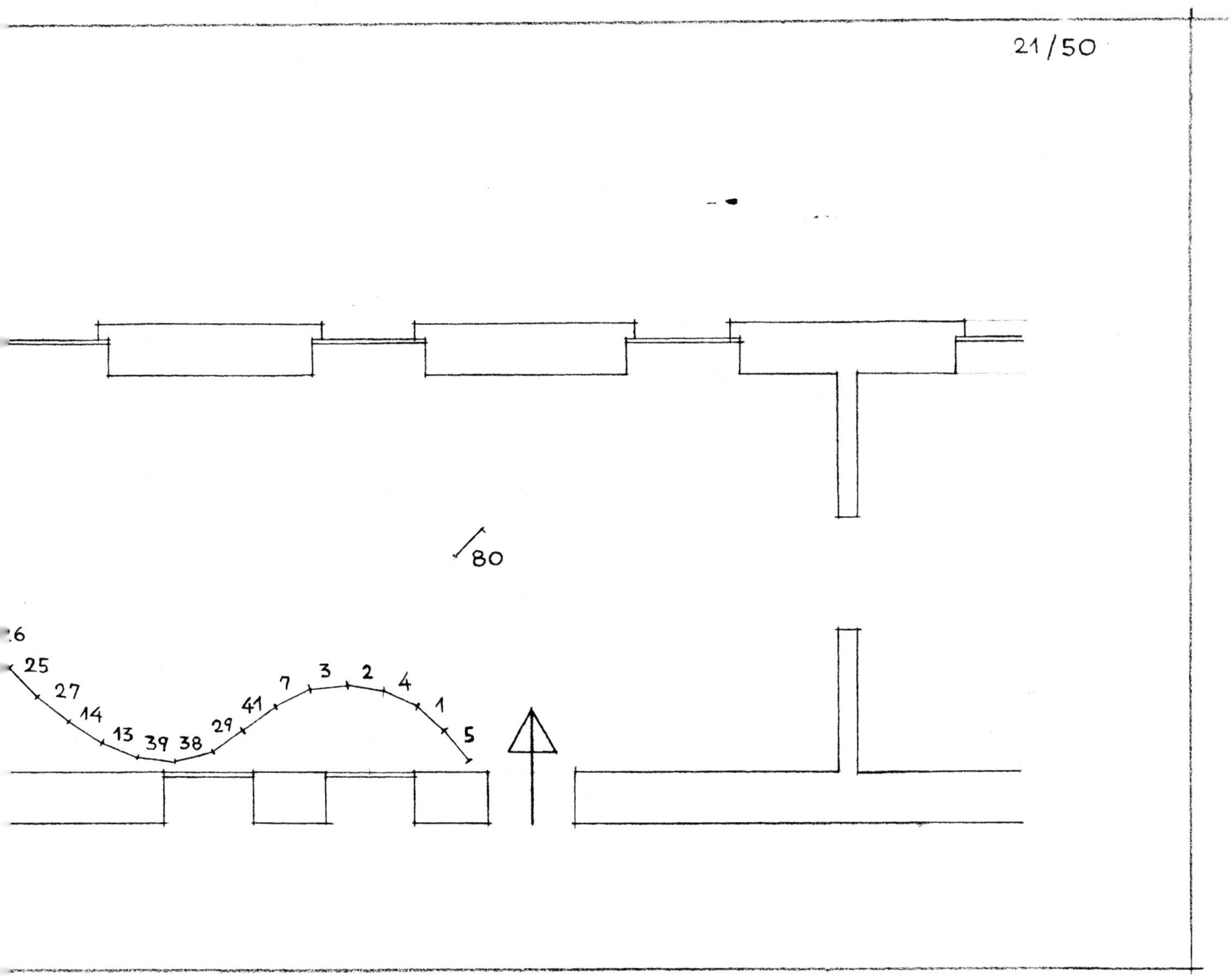

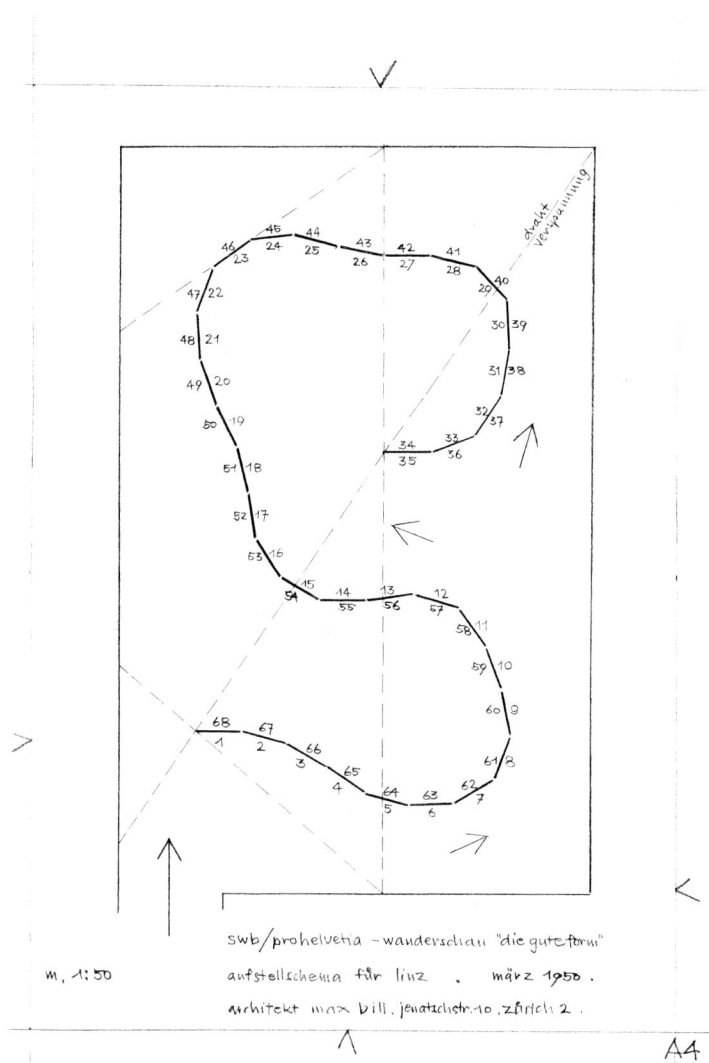

Layout plan for Linz and Graz, 1950.

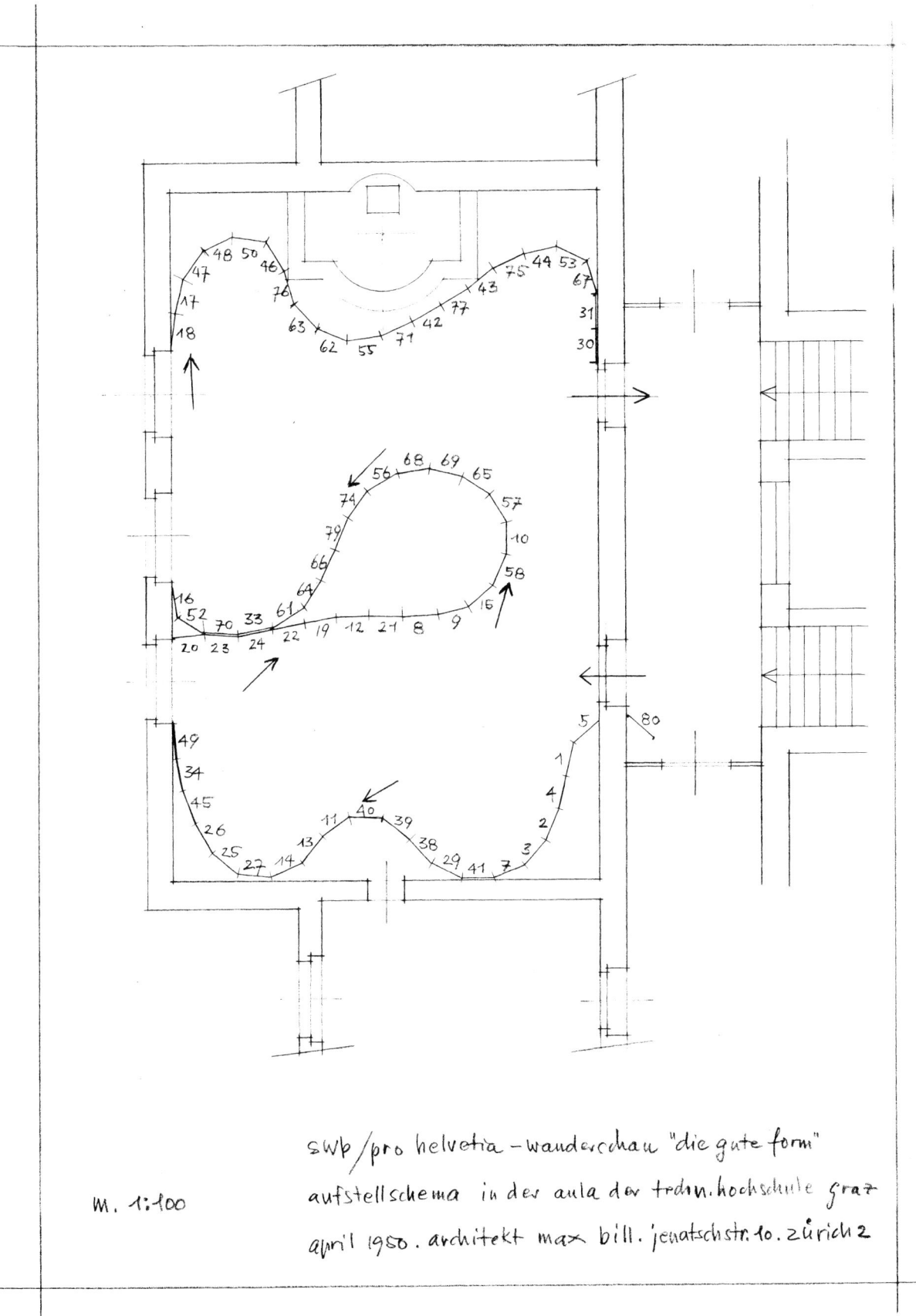

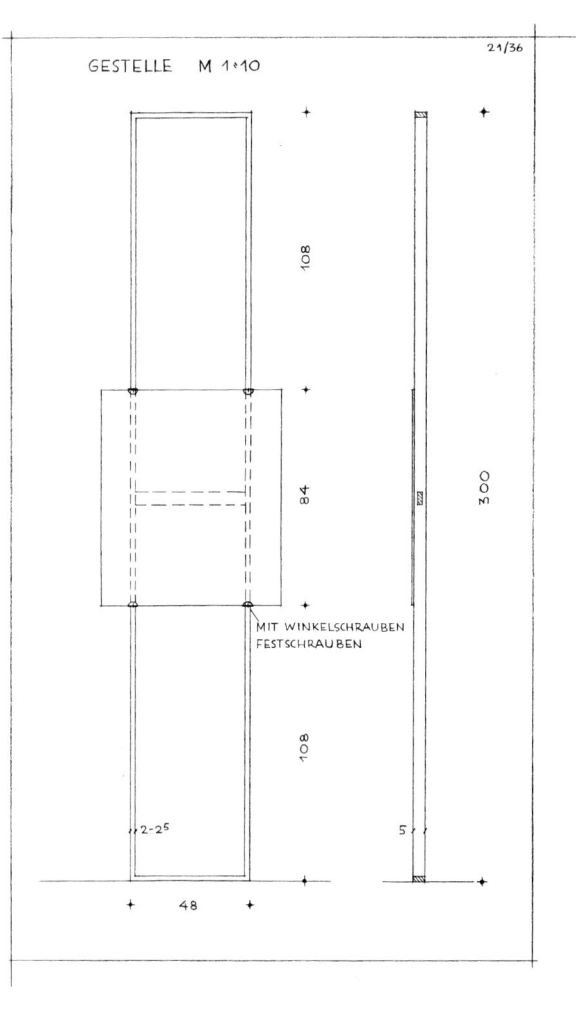

Construction drawing of a frame for the display panels, front and side view, 1949.

Max Bill's construction plan for the entrance wall with sculpture plinth for the Basel exhibition, 1949.

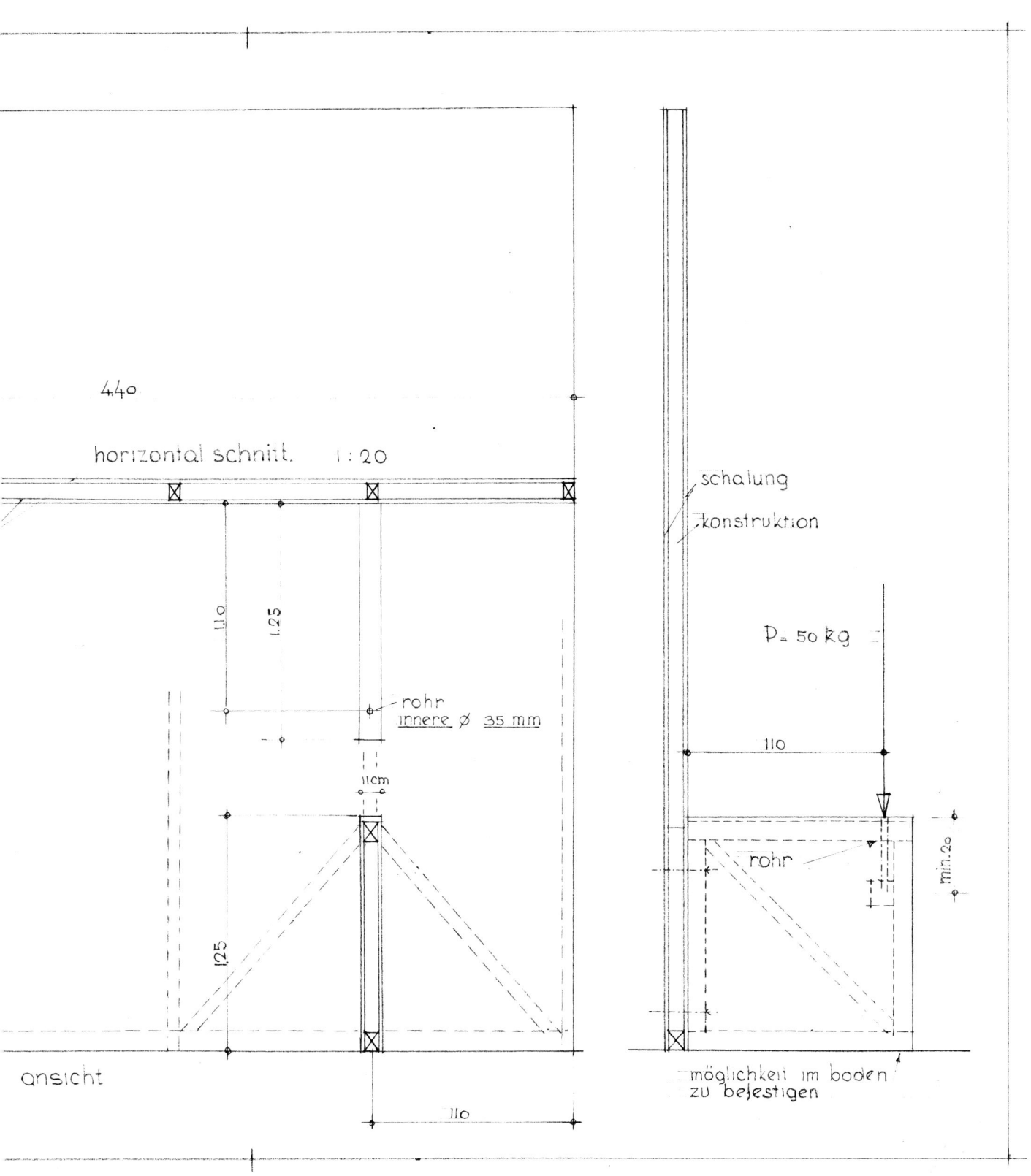

beauty from function and as function
max bill

lecture given on 23 october 1948 at the swiss werkbund annual conference in basel.
reproduced in: *werk,* 8/1949, pp. 272–282

for around a hundred years now the call to arms has sounded through the world in successive waves: we have a duty to make useful, ethical products that are true to materials and manufactured under socially responsible conditions, using the best means available to us. inherent within this call is a sense of moral responsibility, a social understanding. yet in almost every case this is not the starting point but rather the post-rationalisation for a distinctly artistic process. a closer look reveals that the initial impulse arises not so much from a conscious sense of responsibility towards the user as from a feeling of responsibility for the form, from the constant will to define a new expression. the concept of social responsibility is something that artists and others deploy after the event, as a way of justifying their search for new forms corresponding to new or changed conditions.

and that's how it has remained up to the present day, to some extent in technology as well. new forms that are perceived to be artistic arise not out of a pure sense of responsibility towards the eventual user, but out of a more universal need to give things form. this does not mean, of course, that social factors are not taken into account in the design; it's just that such considerations haven't yet been the basis for creating anything.

and so we've reached the point where every change in form— and not just those which can be seen from season to season and influence everyday use-objects as well—can be characterised as a change in social practices and therefore, broadly, as fashion.

now the werkbund has always been associated with the idea of 'truth to materials'. but when we ask ourselves what this phrase really means, it's hard to come up with a definitive answer. we discover that truth to materials depends very much on the fulfilling of function. on the other hand, as everyone knows, almost any form can be produced from almost any material, and it's impossible to say categorically that one variant is 'true' and the other 'false'. to give an example: is it being true to materials to insist that plain ceramics should be of perfect quality when we know this is hard to achieve in terms of production, and certainly much more expensive than the standard process which allows for minor, inconsequential technical flaws?

this makes us realise that what we're actually striving for is something quite different—namely, an extreme utilisation of materials, where the maximum effect is achieved with the minimum of materials. for example, we can construct a tower 300 metres high (the eiffel tower) and make it so light (as eiffel did) that if its height were reduced by a factor of one thousandth, ie by 30 centimetres, then its weight would drop by just 7 grams—the weight of a pencil. this is a shining exemplar of the extreme exploitation of materials, an emblem for the technical age and the rational use of materials, as well as the germ of a new ideal of beauty. this coupling of the engineer's rationalism with beauty in construction—or 'rational beauty', as henry van de velde put it in his day—is the banner under which we must regroup when considering how to tackle production both now and in the future.

beauty from function—which we still consider an essential codeterminant of beauty as function—is a phenomenon most readily observed when functions are brought to light in the purest way, without sentimental frippery, that is, in the construction of machines and tools, in the work of the engineer, though even here we can observe that forms often change in response to contemporary tastes while the functions remain the same.

this fact—that engineered forms change not only in response to changes in function but also for aesthetic reasons—is evidence of the tight correlation between beauty from function and beauty as function. regrettably, however, this aesthetic insight seems barely to have penetrated the parallel field of everyday use objects.

for years we've been asking how this has come about. for years, for generations now, the werkbund has been stating its demands clearly, with less than satisfactory results. you have to search long and hard to find a simple, functional and beautiful chair, beautiful crockery, a functional, all-purpose door handle, a functional and beautiful lamp. it has become clear to us that beauty can no longer be developed out of function alone; instead, the demand for beauty has to be set on the same level as a functional demand, since it is a function too.

if we place particular value on something being beautiful, it's because pure functionality, in its narrow sense, is not what concerns us in the long term. we should no longer have to demand functionality—it ought to be a matter of course. but beauty is less self-evident, and ideas about what is beautiful or not beautiful often differ. that's why it's easier to keep on calling for functionality. the pursuit of beauty is much more difficult; it requires a greater effort, and succeeds only under particular creative conditions, when the idea of form meshes harmoniously with the particular task in hand. the two preconditions for this are first, the right commission, and second, the competence to design.

let's first consider the commission before moving on to the question of the competence to design.

we are all know that commissions have the potential to oppress. when we're given a brief to design something with a 'classic' status—for example, the constant tea cup, the one true chair, the definitive coffee pot, the folding step that can be deployed in any situation—we're fully aware of the relative nature of our products' claims to 'eternal' value. but it would be remiss to lessen our efforts to achieve the definitive result—or what corresponds at that moment, under those particular conditions, to our ideal of beauty—just because we know that, no matter what, this ideal is bound to change. we know that in every area of the production of use goods, which includes the house itself as well as cars, trains and ships, there are an infinite number of projects that we could apply ourselves to with the aim of making something better and more beautiful than the things that already exist.

a great deal of effort has already gone into spelling out to manufacturers the need for beautifully designed products. we do not distinguish here between the handcrafted and the industrially manufactured product, since both require our input. if we nonetheless place an emphasis on industrial goods, it's because these are manufactured in larger quantities and so have a much greater cultural impact than individual pieces. however, when we come to take stock of what our efforts have achieved up to now, it seems we've made little progress.

the reason for this lies in part with the nature of the swiss economy. in making his decisions the swiss manufacturer tends to have one eye on fashion trends abroad and the other on his immediate economic situation. in times of full employment he is reluctant to introduce new models, since this would disrupt the manufacturing process—even though this is precisely the moment he could afford to do so. when business is slow, on the other hand, he feels less committed to maintaining the technical quality of his products. socially responsible manufacturers now have the possibility—indeed even the duty—to make products that are exemplary not only technically, but also formally. but it has to be said that very few of them have given this any thought, and despite our efforts many of them don't even know how to begin to tackle this problem.

i believe that the path the werkbund has pursued up to now is perhaps not the right one, since we've failed to reach the circles that matter in switzerland. i believe we could get better results from the approach, proposed a long time ago, of highlighting the cultural aspects of production through special exhibitions of exemplary products at trade fairs. this would increase awareness among influential people. as you know, the leipzig fair put on exhibitions of this kind for many years, which worked well because manufacturers saw it as an honour to have their products selected for a showcase for quality, run by people who knew what they were doing.

finally, i have a few more remarks to make on the question of who is qualified to create industrial products. the past few years have seen the emergence of a new profession, the 'industrial designer', as they call it in anglo-saxon countries, where it's more prevalent than it is here, in some cases taking on corporate dimensions. much of what these designers produce looks very attractive, and is superficially modern, but the design is often substandard, wantonly frivolous, with the fine facade concealing technical problems. in this way a new style is being propagated and mass-produced. it is being 'streamlined'.

so today's streamlined car bodies are in many cases the product of pure formalism, while insights that were ignored for many years—while paul jaray still had a patent on their pure form—are now being embraced for the sake of fashion. the result: the production of inflated tin cans—massive, but not significantly more comfortable—that are already shrinking our streets and parking places in a most unpleasant way. from cars it's then a natural step to extend this 'streamlining' to household appliances, prams and radios. but thankfully this epidemic has barely touched swiss industry.

here in switzerland everything proceeds at a slightly more leisurely pace. for a start, things of beauty tend to be viewed with some suspicion in our puritanical and censorious land. but it can hardly be assumed this will always be so. sooner or later developments that start abroad begin to percolate into switzerland. the 'industrial designer' will arrive here too: just as the commercial graphic designer evolved from the painter who engaged with graphics into the independent profession of today, so the industrial designer will evolve out of necessity. but going by the dispiriting examples we've seen from abroad, these designers pose a substantial threat to our chances of checking the move towards superficiality. this is why we also have to ask: how do these designers enter the profession, and what are the demands that the werkbund must make of them?

let's consider why industrial designers might be a good thing: mass production has to ensure not only that a certain beauty arises from the function of consumer goods, but that this beauty itself becomes a function. in the future, mass-market consumer goods will be the barometer for a country's cultural standing. the designers of these goods will ultimately be responsible for a large part of our visual culture, just as architects are responsible for the healthy development of our cities and living places. the kind of practice we envisage, with its vast range of responsibilities, requires us to make quite different demands of the industrial designer than were made, for example, of designers of applied arts in the early days of industrialisation. we are facing an educational problem which is perhaps not very significant on an individual level, but is exceptionally important in terms of its cultural impact—an educational problem that we'd scarcely begun to address at the time of the bauhaus and that is hardly resolved today. there are no schools giving people the kind of education that we require today, no school producing people that we could employ without reservation for this important task.

in switzerland, to date, there has been not a single move in this direction. even if you are of the opinion that our technical colleges (*gewerbeschulen*) and schools of industrial arts (*kunstgewerbeschulen*) are potentially the right kind of institution, it has to be said that they're quite unsuited to this purpose in their current form. since the education provided by a technical college has broadly to comply with swiss laws on the training of apprentices, it's not much different from a practical apprenticeship, and there are plenty who maintain that the education on offer is incomplete.

but if on-the-job training is in many cases more or less equivalent to completing a course at college, what's the point of college? what can it offer that's special, rather than generally available? only specialist subjects, suitable for those pursuing a vocational training, still seem to be justified, whereas the craft taught in colleges today is biased towards the arts as a whole. schools of industrial arts that work with a curriculum that is not substantially different from vocational training have lost their primary function, the purpose they were set up for, which is to point the way forward for progressive industry.

i've already remarked that there's essentially no difference between industry and handcraft, that the machine is a tool in the same way that a hammer is, for example, that these are simply the prostheses we create to implement our work. nonetheless, today there is still a large manual element in what we call industrial production. products that appear to be technical are still made using relatively craft-based methods. so if i reproach the schools of industrial arts for still being mostly craft-based, i'm not saying that they should ignore these techniques, but rather that they're not thinking enough about industry.

i believe there's no need to reiterate why industry is so important today. unless you're cut off from reality you can't fail to see that in the long term industrial development offers not just a huge opportunity for cultural development but also a means of freeing people from the burden of heavy labour. clearly, both of these things have yet to come about, but if we want to develop our cultural potential we need to have competent people making these industrial products—hence the necessity to educate this kind of designer. this represents a major challenge for our schools of industrial arts, not in their current form and with their current curriculum, but more as the foundation for something new. based on my experience, i will briefly sketch out what such an education ought to look like.

student numbers have to be kept very low. the prerequisite for study should be the completion of a technical apprenticeship, or possibly an equivalent course at a school of industrial arts, with a final examination in a technical subject. students would not only get a comprehensive training giving them an insight into all the related professions, and with this a feeling for new materials, they'd also get a general education encompassing theory and practice in all fields of design as well as the basic concepts of statics, mechanics and physics. they would have to work with all kinds of material, not only theoretically but also in practical exercises carried out in workshops under appropriate supervision; in short, on top of their basic craft-based training they would receive a very complete artistic, technical and intellectual education. it is clear that such an institution cannot be constructed along the same lines as existing schools of industrial arts but has to be much more a kind of hybrid between an academy and a polytechnic, as the bauhaus set out to be. a much greater emphasis, however, has to be placed on the development of personality: what we need are designers who are not just technically knowledgeable but are also true artists, uninfected by the idea that painting or making sculptures is somehow more important or of greater value than making perfectly beautiful, good industrial products.

only when the production of mass-market consumer goods gets into the hands of such people will we be able to say that the cultural epoch of the machine age has truly begun. until then, everything will remain piecemeal, at the mercy of chance.

so while we have to acknowledge, with regret, that our efforts have not yet yielded substantial results and large-scale production has not yet reached the standard we'd hoped for, we also have to accept that it will not be so easy to reach this standard any time soon, given the lack of an appropriate skills base.

to reiterate: our future industrial designers should not see their work as being less valuable than that of painters or sculptors. this does not constitute a declaration of war on the fine arts, for just as the latest discoveries in theoretical physics are ultimately indispensable for the production of simpler, more practical appliances that are of greater use to everyone, so the fine arts are indispensable for the development of all sorts of objects, and it is absolutely essential to grapple not only with the art of the past but also with the latest contemporary issues. doing so will give a certain stylistic cohesion to all our diverse efforts, a unity between the latent formal tendencies and the explicit and unequivocal function of fine art, which is to bring forth perfect beauty, unimpaired by external constraints or restrictions. in this context, art also gives us a glimpse of the possibilities and questions, both positive and negative, that are in the air at any one time. confronting these problems of design, which are now presenting themselves in a crystalline form, is not only essential in the production of use-objects, it's also an existential question of the first order for architecture. unless it engages positively with these questions—and goes beyond treating mural painting and sculpture as decorative accessories – architecture, just like industrial design, will never get beyond a primitive stage of satisfying needs and instead lose its way in historicist and artistic games.

whatever we're looking at—appliances, shoes, technical tools or contemporary artworks—we can see a certain stylistic unity begin to emerge, a unity that does not depend on the addition of external elements, in contrast to the 'style' envisaged by one particularly doughty housewife when she lectured adolf loos on the subject: 'if the bedside table has a lion's head on it and this lion's head also features on the sofa, the wardrobe, the beds, the armchairs, the washstand, in short on all the objects in the room, now that's what you call style'. but that's not the kind of style i mean; what i'm talking about is something that arises out of a disciplined, purposeful approach to design. we can draw a certain satisfaction from much of what we're doing today, and while concrete results may still be thin on the ground, there are enough of them to give us hope that the path we've embarked on is not misguided, and that this development will lead somewhere. these results also show that our thesis, which is now being taken up with renewed vigour, can be the basis for building a new culture that corresponds to our potential and our aesthetic conceptions. that this will need time to come about is something that has become clear to us over the course of the years.

our efforts today have to go in two directions: first, into making manufacturers aware of the issues and increasing their awareness of their cultural responsibility, and secondly, into giving suitably talented individuals an education that will allow them, as industrial designers, to draw on their own experience, their own outlook and their own sense of responsibility to create things that we will be happy to use all the time, everyday—all kinds of things from a sewing needle to the arrangement of a house, and all of them guided by a spirit of beauty which is developed from function and which, through its beauty, fulfils its own function.

Translation by Pamela Johnston, published in *Architecture Words* 5, 2010, p. 32–41.

good form

max bill

exhibition guide no. 183, zurich kunstgewerbemuseum, 1950

this travelling exhibition [*die gute form*] highlights outstanding achievements in the most varied fields of human activity, ranging from pure observations of particularly perfect natural formations, through scientific discoveries, to products derived from artistic intuition—from a creative impulse which then finds its parallel in the application of natural laws to technology at all scales, from machine components to household appliances to the sophisticated work-tools used by people today.

all of these forms arise from more or less exact thought processes. most are based on extensive experience and are the outcome of long years of development. but this is not the case with all the things that surround us. many of these are shaped by completely different motives, since development is not a linear process. thus a stool—to take as an example one of our simplest, most essential use objects—is not always determined by purely functional needs; in fact, whether any stool is truly functional in the real sense of the word—satisfying all requirements for comfort and elegance while at the same time being affordable—is highly debatable. meanwhile, people go on making stools in the form of ship's propellers, for example.

curiously, the serviceability of a stool is harder to gauge than the increased efficiency of a new machine. something else comes into play when we evaluate things, and that something else is what is (rather generally) called 'beauty'.

there is an old saying that beauty is in the eye of the beholder, and that taste is a personal matter. but experience shows that it is perfectly possible to talk about taste. some things are widely considered to be beautiful, others are seen as ugly. to some extent, this is tied to how old the things are. with objects that are subject to technical change, ie when their function is not yet fully developed, the form ages rather quickly. a telephone from 25 years ago may look like an oddity today. and a 40-year-old car comes across as a joke, unless you happen to be an aficionado assessing it from a technical viewpoint. at the beginning of the twentieth century, appliances like cookers or sewing machines were still quite primitive, and people felt had they to be decked with scrolls.

items of furniture are a different matter, because their function is fundamentally unchanged and their development essentially complete, even if certain changes occur in their use and in the technical possibilities of manufacture. in such cases changes arise not on account of function but as a result of shifting tastes. the role of age is then reversed: what is old now becomes beautiful: customs, memories of the bygone splendour of the landed gentry, the yearning to return to the way things used to be, all become confused with the inherent value of the things. the more ostentatious something is, the more people seem to want it. the striving for a higher station in life, the desire for social advancement, often finds expression in misguided extravagance. but don't we also have the saying 'appearances can be deceptive'? and isn't this borne out by experience? that's why we've tried in this exhibition to dispense as much as possible with 'appearance' and focus instead on what is modest, true— even good.

but now let's get back to taste—a disputed area—and to the fact that many other factors apart from taste determine the form of an object. one of these is the material employed, whether it is solid or unsound. another is whether the object is practical or barely usable. or whether it corresponds to its purpose perfectly, or only partially. or obstructs space, or frees it up. or how much it costs in relation to its true value, ie whether it's good value or overpriced. these are all rational arguments that we take into account when we buy an object, or at least that we ought to factor in; and together these arguments shape our perception of quality. we learn from experience that quality is never cheap, though it turns out to be the cheapest option in the long run, and that its outer form is mostly simple, low-key.

if we do not take these qualities into account when making our purchases, we are led by something else: namely by the way things look, their external appearance. but just because something looks expensive, it doesn't necessarily mean it has any value. a sleek veneer tends to conceal a lack of true quality. true quality is usually defined by an unostentatious elegance. so we're justified in mistrusting the outer appearance, which can take on a number of guises—which can lie. these guises are not only plucked from the past, they don't just mimic styles from the gothic to constructivism: there's also a contemporary version of this masquerade—the streamlined style. and there are good grounds for mistrusting this too. it's a fashion that bears as little relation to contemporary realities as a style from the past. streamlined, or empire style—both are equally ridiculous when applied to a pram. both would have the pram appear as something other than it really is. both lie.

by contrast, what our exhibition aims to present are projects that are sincere and in keeping with the spirit of our times. we already know that things of perfection arise only rarely— propelled by vanity, people can't leave a simple thing alone; they always have to add something to make it stand out. and when this is done with a measure of skill and good sense, we begin to believe that it's possible to add a touch of individuality, of, let's say, artistic intuition—that it's possible to take an object of straightforward construction and make it beautiful too, consciously beautiful. but things like this are even rarer than things which fulfil their purpose in a good, straightforward way: ie machines, work-tools, appliances. hence we can already count ourselves fortunate if the things that we use everyday serve people in the same manner as work-tools, rather than offending reason. some people may object that such expectations are not realistic, that people are not rational but will always judge things according to their own vague notion of taste. yet experience teaches us that this is not quite the case. though we know that people's habits change only slowly, we can still observe a change in taste occurring over time, so that many things that would have been thought beautiful 40 years ago are now seen as ridiculously florid and overdone. equally, many of the things that appear experimental today will tomorrow seem quite normal.

it is often asked whether we need to continue to make things in the time-honoured manner, or alternatively convert wholesale to 'industrial' production. this question is only of hypothetical interest. our concern here is to make available to a large number of people things that are as beautiful as they can be—and good value. both traditional crafts and industry are in a position to fulfil this wish, as there is in principle no difference between these manufacturing techniques when it comes to producing quality.

if the focus here is almost exclusively on furnishing objects, it's because these are of particular concern to the swiss werkbund. no less important, however, are buildings: they have to last even longer, and we have to be happy living in them for many years. the face of our cities, our towns and villages, our landscape is likewise a concern, for this bears witness to our era's capabilities—or lack of them—not only today and tomorrow but for generations to come.

so if we've tried to allude to all of these issues in our exhibition by presenting selected, complementary examples from the most diverse creative fields, we do so out of a desire to highlight the forces that are making a positive contribution to shaping the face of the present. and if we close with the remark that the future will judge our time in the same way that we judge the past, that is, according to its cultural character and the cultural level it has reached, as well as by its social achievements, then we must guard ourselves against the danger of going by appearances and instead attempt to bring all our contemporary powers into a harmonious balance—into what we'd like to call 'good form'.

Translation by Pamela Johnston, published in *Architecture Words* 5, 2010, p. 28–31.

the conditions of work over the period of *die gute form*

jakob bill

the fact that that max bill had to create the exhibition *die gute form* within a very short period of time is all the more remarkable when we look at his work schedule over this same period and at the raft of other projects on which he was concurrently involved.

in 1948 max bill was still working entirely from home, in the house and studio he had built in 1932/33 in zurich's höngg[1] district. with the finalization of the commission for *die gute form,* however, and the volume of work now facing him within such a tight deadline, bill not only had to turn down an invitation from josef albers, who had offered him in 1949 a guest lectureship at black mountain college in north carolina, but also look for new office space.

since the house in höngg was too small to accommodate assistants, at the start of 1949 bill rented an office at 10 jenatschstrasse in zurich's enge district, which he proceeded to furnish in the simplest manner for the time being. as from february 1 the new, centrally-located premises were ready for use as an office for architecture and product design.[2] a secretary was also employed. this enabled bill to pursue several projects at once, delegate the correspondence related to the exhibition, and supervise the assembly of the display panels on-site.

the official go-ahead for the exhibition *die gute form* was evidently given at a meeting of the swb exhibition committee on january 21, 1949. between then and the next meeting on february 10, max bill prepared an estimate of costs. the swb then had to obtain the necessary funding—a process that, in turn, took time. since the swb wanted to invite its members itself, bill's hands were tied with regard to sending out binding requests within switzerland. he was nevertheless able to start making enquiries abroad for photos of objects that matched his criteria. in order to find out the addresses of people to contact and so build up a network, on february 25 a number of letters written in english were sent by airmail to london, chicago, and new york. the following day a french version of the letter was posted to paris. replies were not long in arriving.

during these same weeks bill was also working intensively on the preparations for the exhibition *pevsner—vantongerloo—bill* for kunsthaus zürich, which was due to open in april.[3] he also organized the exhibition *zürcher konkrete kunst* (poster and catalog), which was shown in stuttgart, munich, and braunschweig. in his parallel capacity as architect, bill designed a commercial and residential apartment building for anton aicher[4] in the söflingen district of ulm; the plans drawn up by bill are all dated february 22, 1949 and were submitted to the ulm planning department just over three weeks later on march 16. at the same time, bill draw up a proposal for a "municipal hall with stage," following a call for competition entries in december 1948 by the swiss town of grenchen; these had to be submitted by march 31. bill was also heavily involved in a number of writing projects: his article on the "haus für ein künstlerpaar in ascona" was imminently due to appear,[5] along with his monograph on the Swiss bridge engineer robert maillart[6]—the first of its kind—and his portfolio *moderne schweizer architektur.*[7]

on march 5 the swb announced that the swiss department of the interior had approved a grant of 20,000 francs to install the first version of the exhibition at the basel mustermesse trade fair. funding for the second version, which was to tour germany, was not yet secured, however. on march 23 max bill contacted the german werkbund, which was making preparations for its the *neues wohnen* exhibition in cologne. on march 24 the swb applied for a grant from the swiss arts association pro helvetia. on march 28 bill had to send in an explanatory supporting letter, whereupon 6,000 francs were pledged on march 31. that same day, bill received a quote for the printing of 60,000 exhibition guides, which were to be given out to visitors and to those who had supplied the pictures.[8]

in his capacity as a poster designer, during this period max bill produced posters advertising the june festival weeks for zurich's three main concert halls and theaters, the schauspielhaus, tonhalle, and stadttheater.[9] these posters bore the zurich tourist office's new logo (three seagulls), also developed by him. he likewise designed the poster for the summer *bonnard* exhibition at kunsthaus zürich.[10] not long afterwards his book on *wassily kandinsky* was published by holbein.[11] on april 2 things had progressed to the point where the swb was able to issue invitations to take part in the exhibition *die gute form.* on april 4 a letter from max bill was sent to some 40 swiss firms and manufacturers, asking them to provide good-quality photographs of a specific size. identical letters continued to be sent out up to april 14. following the arrival of suitable images, the corresponding texts were written, and on april 25 the first batch was sent off to the typographer and typesetter emil ruder in basel with the instructions "poem setting". futher texts continued to be delivered up to may 4. the final texts for the german traveling exhibition went to press on may 8. on april 26 bill's office ordered the wooden frames and the entrance wall for the exhibition—for which it also supplied the design drawings—from the basel-based carpentry company zimmereigeschäft und bauschreinerei e. eisenhut ag. the small metal plates today affixed to the panels were not ordered until mid-june and so could only be added after the exhibition had already been to basel and cologne. these chrome-plated brass plates are not visible in the photos of the constance exhibition, suggesting that only the swiss series received them.

at the opening in basel on may 7, max bill personally gave a tour of the exhibition at 3 p.m. the second version opened on may 14 in cologne, albeit without max bill; werner schmalenbach was present, however, and on may 19 wrote a report of the show for the swb.

1 arthur rüegg (ed.), *das atelierhaus max bill 1932/33* (sulgen, 1997).

2 in this year bill designed his three-legged stool, "three-round table," and "square round table."

3 for reasons of time and money, the exhibition was put back to autumn (october 15–november 13, 1949). max bill wrote his subsequently much-cited essay "die mathematische denkweise in der kunst unserer zeit" (the mathematical way of thinking in the art of our time) for the catalog.

4 anton aicher was the father of otl aicher. inge scholl and otl aicher visited max bill for the first time in 1948 and initially wanted to engage him as a lecturer at their adult education college in ulm. there followed an intensive exchange of ideas, during which the proposal for a "school of design" took concrete shape. they continued to correspond on the subject in spring 1949, the period that interests us here. scholl and aicher hosted *die gute form* in ulm.

5 max bill, "haus für ein künstlerpaar in ascona," in *bauen und wohnen* 5 (1949), pp. 65–66. jakob bill, "due progetti architettonici in ticino/zwei architekturprojekte im tessin," in riccardo carazzetti (ed.), *100 max bill,* exh. cat. pinacoteca comunale casa rusca, locarno (2008), pp. 54–75.

6 max bill, *robert maillart* (erlenbach, 1949).

7 max bill (ed.), *moderne schweizer architektur 1925–1945* (basel, 1949).

8 the fact that an estimate could be prepared means that the exhibition guide, which took the form of an illustrated booklet, must already have been finished in broad outline.

9 max bill, *typografie—reklame—buchgestaltung* (sulgen, 1999), p. 224.

10 ibid., p. 225.

11 max bill, *wassily kandinsky,* 10 color reproductions (basel, 1949).

title	basel 1949	list 20/1/50	zhdk-inv-no A-Werkbund-	vienna 1950	linz 1950	graz 1950	zurich 1950	second-number	amsterdam 1951
empty		1							
empty		2							
empty		3							
empty		5							
movements	8	1	0001	2	3	3	2	3	3
mathematics represented in space	10	2	0002	4	5	5	4	5	5
sculptural art	11	3	0003	5	6	6	5	6	6
the limits of the visible	9	4	0004	3	4	4	3	4	4
matter in its highest form	6	5	0005	1	2	2	1	2	2
flow forms	7	6	0006					0	
sculptural art	12	7	0007	6	7	7	6	7	7
educational institutions	28	8	0008	39	42	29	32	35	35
universities	29	9	0009	40	43	30	33	36	36
concrete construction elements	32	10	0010	44	46	33	35	38	38
bridges	33	11	0011	43	13	13	13	8	
office buildings	26	12	0012	37	40	27	29	32	32
stylistic unity in technology	35	13	0013	11	14	14	14	9	9
high-voltage power line masts	34	14	0014	12	15	15	16	11	11
medical buildings	30	15	0015	41	44	31	30	33	33
bathroom fittings	39	16	0016	26	29	47	53	44	44
light switches and plugs	41	17	0017	24	27	49	51	42	42
bathroom faucets	40	18	0018	25	28	48	52	43	43
housing ensembles	25	19	0019	36	39	26	37	30	30
national and regional planning	21	20	0020	32	35	22	25	26	26
the classroom	27	21	0021	38	41	28	31	34	34
differentiated residential neighborhoods	24	22	0022	35	38	25	28	29	29
city planning	22	23	0023	33	36	23	26	27	27
planned towns	23	24	0024	34	37	24	27	28	28
train cars	78	25	0025	14	17	17	20	21	21
airplanes	80	26	0026	15	18	18	21	22	22
rail cars	79	27	0027	13	16	16	19	20	20
rail buses	77	28	0028					0	
machine forms	14	29	0029	8	9	9	18	13	13
typewriters	75	30	0030	21	24	67	11	18	18
office devices	74	31	0031	20	23	66	12	19	19
audio transmission		32	0032	17	20			0	
hanging lamps	42	33	0033	22	25	44	47	60	60
image transmission		34	0034	18	21	20	23	24	24
standard components	37	35	0035	46			49	40	40
handles	20	36	0036					0	
scales	17	37	0037				10	17	17
magnifying instruments	18	38	0038	9	10	10	7	14	14
technicians' tools	19	39	0039	10	11	11	8	15	15
measuring devices	16	40	0040		12	12	9	16	16
technological forms	13	41	0041	7	8	8	17	12	12
toiletries	68	42	0042	61	62	59	68	69	69
wristwatches	69	43	0043	63	64	61	70	71	71
men's shoes	73	44	0044	65	66	63	72	73	73
automobiles	76	45	0045	16	19	19	22	23	23
unambiguous utensil forms	56	46	0046	31	34	53	60	51	51
kitchen tools	59	47	0047	28	31	50	55	46	46
cookware	60	48	0048	29	32	51	56	47	47
radio receivers		49	0049	19	22	21	24	25	25
household appliances	57	50	0050	30	33	52	59	50	50
kitchen accessories	58	51	0051				58	49	49
kitchen furnishings	38	52	0052	27	30	46	54	45	45
garden living	53	53	0053	66	67	64	65	66	66
combination tables	44	54	0054					0	
bowls and containers	66	55	0055	59	60	57	64	65	65
plywood and laminated wood chairs	47	56	0056	50	51	38	40	53	53
prefabricated buildings	36	57	0057	45	47	34	36	39	39
reinforced concrete buildings	31	58	0058	42	45	32	34	37	37
privacy and sun shades	54	59	0059				50	41	41
electrical engineering	15	60	0060				15	10	10
tea tables	46	61	0061	55	56	43	46	59	59
drinking glasses	63	62	0062	58	59	56	63	64	64
coffee and tea services	62	63	0063	57	58	55	62	63	63
serving tables	45	64	0064	54	55	42	45	58	58
living rooms	52	65	0065	47	48	35		31	31
easy chairs	50	66	0066	53	54	41	44	57	57
toys	65	67	0067	67	68	65	66	67	67
prefabricated furniture	55	68	0068	49	50	37	39	52	52
living rooms		69	0069	48	49	36	38	0	
table lamps	43	70	0070	23	26	45	48	61	61
decorative forms	67	71	0071	60	61	58	67	68	68
rainwear	71	72	0072					0	
beds and daybeds	51	73	0073				43	56	56
woven-strap chairs	48	74	0074	51	52	39	41	54	54
women's shoes	72	75	0075	64	65	52	71	72	72
porcelain dishware	61	76	0076	56	57	54	61	62	62
jewelry	70	77	0077	62	63	60	69	70	70
coffeemakers	64	78	0078				57	48	48
armchairs	49	79	0079	52	53	40	42	55	55
introduction panel	4	80	0080	0	1	1		0	1
selection of swiss goods		81	0081					0	

chapter 1
chapter 2
chapter 3
chapter 4
unused plates

Table of the panel configurations at various exhibition venues, compiled by Jakob Bill.

A selection of around 17 panels from *Die gute Form* were presented at the 1949 Swiss Radio exhibition at the Kongresshaus in Zurich.

Street view in Constance, 1949 (left).
Exhibition at the city hall in Constance (middle, right).

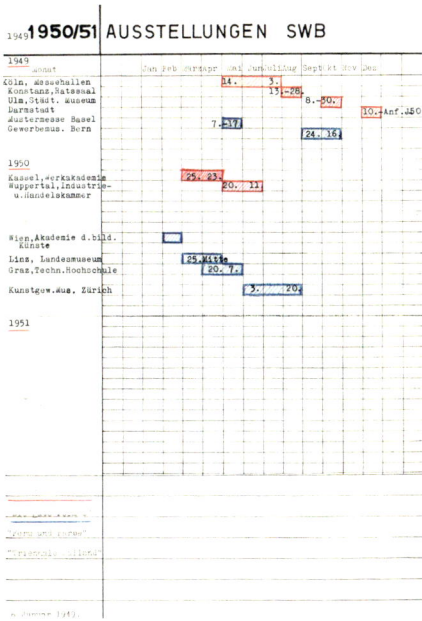

View of the exhibition spaces in Vienna and Linz, 1950.

Time chart drawn up by Max Bill for the different exhibition venues.

151

Chronology

1947

The organizers of the Milan Triennale invite Max Bill to design the entrance hall for the 1947 Triennale. Financial difficulties cause the project to be shelved.

1948

Start of 1948
The Swiss Werkbund (SWB) plans a "didactic travelling exhibition," to be shown in Switzerland and abroad. The SWB thereby aims to counter the prewar nostalgia that is palpable, from a Swiss perspective, in design trends in Germany and Austria with examples of contemporary design.

April 1948
Max Bill submits his proposal for the exhibition "zweck + konstruktion = form" (purpose + construction = design) to the SWB. It is to comprise four sections each featuring 22 panels, namely:
"1. design clearly demonstrating function;
2. design in architecture; 3. design in the home;
4. design in daily life." This concept becomes the basis of Die gute Form.

October 12, 1948
The SWB applies for an exhibition space at the 1949 Basel Mustermesse.

October 23, 1948
Bill gives the lecture "Beauty from function and as function" at the SWB annual conference, for which he earns much criticism from SWB circles. The theme of the conference is the relationship between the economy and design. The director of the Mustermesse, Theodor Brogle, gives a talk on "The notion of quality and design in Swiss industry."

November 1948
The SWB is allocated the Rosenthal gymnasium on the edge of the Mustermesse fair grounds for its exhibition

1949

January 1949
The provisional title of the exhibition is now Funktion und Form (function and design).

March 18, 1949
The Federal Department of the Interior agrees to provide funding for the project. Only now can Bill officially start putting the exhibition into place. The photographer Ernst Scheidegger assists Bill with designing and producing the 80 panels. The typesetting is carried out by Emil Ruder.

May 7–17, 1949
First presentation of Die gute Form at the Swiss Mustermesse, Basel (Series S). The three-dimensional objects – furniture and lighting – are exhibited only in Basel.

Further exhibition locations: "Die gute Form S*"

May 25–30, 1949
Zurich, Kongresshaus (Swiss Radio exhibition, selection of approx. 17 panels)

September 24–end of October, 1949
Bern, Gewerbemuseum

Further exhibition locations: "Die gute Form D"

May 14–July 3, 1949
Cologne, Messehallen

August 13–29, 1949
Constance, Rathaus

October 9–30, 1949
Ulm, Städtisches Museum

1950

1951

The Federal Department of the Interior commissions the Swiss Werkbund to design the Swiss Pavilion at the 9th Milan Triennale (design: Max Bill).

1952

Bill's book *FORM. eine Bilanz der Formentwicklung um die Mitte des XX. Jahrhunderts / A Balance Sheet of Mid-twentieth Century Trends in Design* is published in three languages (G/E/F) by Karl Werner, Basel, as a sort of preliminary conclusion to Bill's preoccupation with the subject. It contains roughly half the examples from *Die gute Form,* complemented by some 30 significant examples from after 1949 – not least a testament to the dynamic creativity of these years.

The prize "Die gute Form SWB" is awarded at the Basel Mustermesse for the first time, and from now on annually until 1968.

February 18–March 10, 1950
Vienna, Akademie der Künste

March 25–mid-April 1950
Linz, Landesmuseum

April 20–May 7, 1950
Graz, Technische Hochschule

June 3–August 20, 1950
Zurich, Kunstgewerbemuseum
(as part of the SWB exhibition)

December 16, 1949–start of 1950
Darmstadt

March 25–April 23, 1950
Kassel, Werksakademie

May 20–June 11, 1950
Wuppertal, Industrie- und Handelskammer**

February 18–March 10, 1951
Amsterdam, Stedelijk Museum

April 7–30, 1951
Eindhoven, Van Abbemuseum

May 5–end of May 1951
Rotterdam, Museum Boijmans Van Beuningen

---

* "Die gute Form S" is the version housed in the ZHdK Design collection
** End of the tour by "Die gute Form D", probably due to the poor state of the panels since Darmstadt

Around the world in eighty plates
Renate Menzi

I first came in contact with *Die gute Form* in the early 1990s. I no longer remember exactly why, but I borrowed a book from the library with the auspicious title *Die gute Form* (by Peter Erni and Lars Müller, 1983), interested at the time, as a "student of the applied arts," chiefly in the objects pictured therein. These things gave the impression of being at once old-fashioned and yet contemporary, and I sensed in them a certain kind of beauty that I would only much later associate with good design. After the book became soaked in orange juice while I was carrying it around in my bag—the library charged me for purchasing a new one—I was allowed to keep my copy with the wavy edges.

In the course of numerous loan requests in the anniversary year 2008, I had the opportunity to scrutinize more closely and with the eyes of a collection curator the original plates assembled by Max Bill for the touring exhibition *Die gute Form* in 1949. The simple styling of the paper-mounted plates of black-and-white photographs with their hand-corrected legends stood in stark contrast to the topicality of the message they conveyed. When the 2006 exhibition *Super Normal,* organized by Jasper Morrison and Naoto Fukosawa, then reignited the discussion on the design of objects for everyday use, it further whetted my enthusiasm for the examples of Swiss design recognized with the title "Gute Form." And thus the normative moral claim of "good" came to be linked to the design of normal, everyday objects: Do they still exist, the good old things, or do they in fact have to be reinvented?

Neither in the book accompanying *Super Normal* nor in the many publications and exhibitions mounted by the Werkbund on the subject of "Gute Form" can a binding definition or authoritative design rules be found. They all rely instead on the didactic power of the visual analogy and therefore work with exemplary models of good design. Then, as now, design is taught using images and objects—they are collected, examined, and compared, evaluated and emulated. This requires archives: digital ones such as the Google image search, design blogs, or electronic museums; and material ones such as secondhand shops, design collections, books, and magazines. The Kunstgewerbliche Sammlung (Applied Arts Collection), founded in 1875 even before the establishment of the Kunstgewerbeschule Zürich (School of Applied Arts), still serves as a model collection for education, trade, and industry. Ever since those early days, the Museum für Gestaltung Zürich (Museum of Design) has dedicated itself to the research and communication of design issues. In 1913 it also became the birthplace of the Swiss Werkbund. The Werkbund, in turn, maintains its own "picture collection of good items of everyday use," consisting of loose pages with information written on the back which was mentioned for the first time in the Werkbund's 1963 annual report.

Max Bill most likely used some of the images from this collection for his plates in 1949. However, his cosmos of forms includes far more than just the articles of everyday use that are commonly associated with the label "Die gute Form" primarily due to the annual award that has been conferred by the Swiss Werkbund since 1952. Bill's plates instead convey a more programmatic view of things, which he manages to present as an effectively staged road show. Allowing room for flexible additions and extensions, the plates arranged linearly in space form a winding roller coaster sweeping visitors along through a coherent world of well-designed forms. Organized according to fields of application, the ride combines "high" or "pure forms" from nature, science, and the visual arts with "low" or "functional forms" such as bridges, hospitals, classrooms, living quarters, aircraft, machinery, appliances, furniture—even jewelry and rainwear. The curator justifies his selection with brief commentaries—such as "perhaps the definitive form of an electric light switch"—and provides information on the designers (including several references to himself), producers, and manufacturers. The selection, thematic organization, information, and commentaries reflect Bill's aspirations in a refreshingly uncompromising way. Not to be underestimated here is the contribution made by the medium of photography with its factual perspective, for example in the pictures by Hans Finsler. By eliminating color, scale, and usage context, the relationship of these objects to the everyday world disappears. This magical transformation lends the forms a rock-solid presence: the beauty of "pure form" that Bill discovers in a modern sculpture shows up again as "good design" in the "technical object."

We have three people to thank for the fact that the display plates for the Werkbund's special exhibition *Die gute Form* are today part of the design collection of the Museum für Gestaltung Zürich: Lars Müller discovered the forgotten plates in the attic of the Gewerbemuseum Winterthur (Museum of Applied Arts and Design) and arranged with the museum's conservator at the time, Fritz Hobi, who had rescued them from certain destruction and stored them there, that they should be transferred to the Museum für Gestaltung Zürich under the condition they would be displayed there in a way that was faithful to the original exhibition. This was accordingly done in the exhibition *Gut in Form* in 2001, curated by Claude Lichtenstein.

In 1992 the Swiss Werkbund made a gift to the Design Collection of the 1,700 cards in the Photokartothek (photo card index), with illustrations and information on all the products that received the Gute Form Award, as well as a bundle of exhibition documents. Finally, in 2005, the above-mentioned "picture collection of good items of everyday use" followed as a permanent loan—not least because many of the objects pictured were already in the collection. This meant that the important archival material on *Gute Form* was now accessible in a public archive, an indispensable prerequisite for researching Swiss design history and a golden opportunity for further research, publication, and exhibition projects.

Renate Menzi is the curator of the Design Collection at the Museum für Gestaltung Zürich.

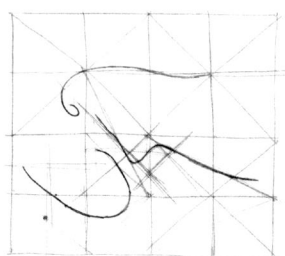

Max Bill, *three colors of equal length*, 1946/47, oil on canvas, 107 × 120 cm.

Max Bill, *unlimited and limited*, 1947, oil on canvas, 110 × 103 cm.

Biography

1908 Max Bill is born on December 22 in Winterthur as the first son of Erwin Bill and Marie Bill-Geiger. Citizen of Moosseedorf (Canton Bern).
1924 Starts training as a silversmith at the Kunstgewerbeschule (School of Applied Arts) in Zurich.
1925 Study trip to Paris, to the *Exposition internationale des arts décoratifs et industriels modernes,* where a selection of his student work is on show. Bill is deeply impressed by Le Corbusier's *Pavillon de l'esprit nouveau,* Friedrich Kiesler's *Raumstadt,* and Konstantin Melnikov's Russian pavilion. First prize in the poster competition celebrating the centenary of the Suchard chocolate factory.
1926 In summer Bill travels to Italy; while there, he produces a series of watercolors. In November he attends a lecture by Le Corbusier in Zurich and forms the idea of studying architecture.
1927 Bill is expelled from the Kunstgewerbeschule for disciplinary reasons following the Fasnacht carnival. On April 20, 1927 he enrols at the Dessau Bauhaus, headed by Walter Gropius. Hannes Meyer sets up a Bauhaus architecture department, which students can join only after a foundation course. Bill completes this preliminary course under Josef Albers and László Moholy-Nagy. Even before he has started studying architecture, Bill submits his first designs for competitions: for the Bern State Library and for a residential and office building in Osaka (in which, as the only European participant, he wins 3rd place). In the winter semester of 1927/28 he trains in the metal workshop under Moholy-Nagy and takes part in Oskar Schlemmer's stage and theater experiments. He attends the free painting classes taught by Wassily Kandinsky and Paul Klee. In summer he takes another study trip to Italy; stays in Positano. On October 30, 1928 Bill leaves Dessau and returns to Switzerland.
1929 Max Bill endeavors to establish himself in Zurich with applied graphics, art and architecture. He writes his "vorschlag eines vorkurses an der kunstgewerbeschule der stadt zürich" ("proposal for a foundation course at the city of zurich school of applied arts"), plans a "uniform und nonstop garage system bill" (a multistory car park in today's terms, but at that time still a utopian concept), and organizes an exhibition of his own works in his apartment-cum-studio.
1930 He adopts the professional name of bill-zürich. Works as a graphic artist, exhibition designer, painter, sculptor, and publicist in the avant-garde circle around Sigfried Giedion. As a designer of posters, adverts, and façade inscriptions, Bill is involved in major Neues Bauen projects in Zurich (Werkbund "Neubühl" housing estate, wohnbedarf furniture store, Zett-Haus building, Corso theater). He becomes a member of the Swiss Werkbund (SWB).
1931 Marries the cellist and photographer Binia Spoerri. Designs the *negerkunst* exhibition poster (Kunstgewerbemuseum, Zurich) and the wohnbedarf company logo; out of this he develops his first three-dimensional work, *wellrelief* (1931/32).
1932/1933 Designs and builds his own home and studio in Zurich's Höngg district (in collaboration with Robert Winkler). Designs the journal *Information* run by Ignazio Silone, a left-wing intellectual organ of the resistance against fascism.
1932–1936 Member of the avant-garde abstraction-création group of artists in Paris; takes part in their actions. Exhibits his first pictures. Contact with Piet Mondrian, Hans Arp, Georges Vantongerloo, and other artists working in a non-figurative abstract vein. Exhibits his first sculptures in Paris.
1934 Designs and builds the Hodel gardener's house in Riehen, just outside Basel.
1935 Contact with Max Ernst and Alberto Giacometti.
1935–1938 Produces his *quinze variations sur un même thème,* published in 1938 as a portfolio of 16 lithographs by Mourlot in Paris.
1936 Designs the Swiss section of the 6th Milan Triennale (awarded the Grand Prix). First plaster version of the sculpture *unendliche schleife* (endless loop). Collaborates on the epoch-making exhibition *Zeitprobleme in der Schweizer Malerei und Plastik* at Kunsthaus Zürich and designs the poster and catalog, publishing in the latter his manifesto on "konkrete gestaltung" ("concrete design").
1937 Joins the *allianz* association of modern Swiss artists. Enters a "Competition for ideas for the design of the shore of Lake Zurich between the concert hall and theater," submitting a concept for a garden city. Project for an architectural tender for a restaurant on Zurich's panoramic Waid hill. Project sketches for the Swiss Pavilion at the 1937 Paris orld's Fair.
1938 Joins the Congrès Internationaux d'Architecture Moderne (CIAM). Editor of *Le Corbusier & Pierre Jeanneret: Œuvre complète 1934–1938,* vol. 3, Zurich, 1939.

1939–1945 Bill is repeatedly called up for military service.
1939 Project sketches for the Swiss Pavilion at the 1939 New York World's Fair. Graphic design of the "Bauen und Planen" section at the Swiss State Exhibition in Zurich.
1940/1941 Project for a competition to design a "Monument to Work" on Zurich's Helvetiaplatz.
1940 Founds the allianz publishing house.
1942 Birth of son Johann Jakob.
1942/1943 Designs and builds the Villiger one-family house in Bremgarten. First use of prefabricated elements made by Durisol.
1944 Designs the publication *Sozialer Wohnungs- und Siedlungsbau,* published by the Delegate for Employment, Zurich. Organizes the first international *konkrete kunst* (concrete art) exhibition at Kunsthalle Basel. Founds the journal *abstrakt/konkret.* Starts working in the field of product design.
1944/1945 Teaches theory of form at the Zurich Kunstgewerbeschule.
1945 Lectures on the subjects of rebuilding, product design, and art in Germany, Italy (takes part in the 1st congress on post-war reconstruction in Milan), and Paris. Publishes the book *Wiederaufbau. Dokumente über Zerstörungen, Planungen, Konstruktionen.* Designs the catalog and poster to the exhibition *USA baut* at the Zurich Kunstgewerbemuseum.
1946/1947 Executes a large-scale version of his sculpture *kontinuität* (continuity) for the Zurich cantonal exhibition of trade and agriculture (destroyed in 1948 in an act of vandalism). Friendship with Henry van de Velde, who settles in Switzerland. Concept for the Swiss contribution to the 8th Milan Triennale (not executed).
1948 At the SWB conference in Basel, Bill delivers his lecture on "Schönheit aus Funktion und als Funktion" ("Beauty from function and as function"), which leads to the project for the exhibition *Die gute Form.*
1949 The exhibition *Die gute Form* is shown at the Mustermesse trade fair in Basel and subsequently travels to other cities in Switzerland, Austria, and the Netherlands. A second version of the same exhibition tours Germany. In the catalog to the Kunsthaus Zürich exhibition *Pevsner – Vantongerloo– Bill,* likewise curated by Bill, he publishes the text "die mathematische denkweise in der kunst unserer zeit" ("the mathematical approach in the art of our time"). Publishes the portfolio *Moderne Schweizer Architektur, Teil II, 1942–47.* Bill becomes a member of the Union des artistes modernes (UAM) in Paris. Publishes the monograph *Robert Maillart.* Project for a "house for an artist couple in Ascona."
1949/1950 Project for a housing estate in Israel using Durisol pre-fabricated components. Project for a pavilion school and multistory apartment buildings in Zurich's Seebach district.
1950–1955 Develops the programme for, plans, and builds the Hochschule für Gestaltung (HfG; Institute of Design) in Ulm. From 1951 to 1956 Bill is also the Institute's first rector and head of the departments of architecture and product design.
1950 First major retrospective of his artistic oeuvre at the Museu de Arte Moderna in São Paulo; goes on to win the Grand Prix for sculpture at the São Paulo Bienal de Arte (1951).
1951 Designs the Swiss Pavilion at the 9th Milan Triennale (awarded the Grand Prix). Project for the competition for the Swiss Pavilion for the Venice Biennale.
1951/1952 Edits the monograph *Wassily Kandinsky* (published by Maeght Editeur in Paris) and Kandinsky's book: *Über das Geistige in der Kunst* (4th edition).
1952 Publishes the book *Form: eine bilanz über die formentwicklung um die mitte des XX. jahrhunderts / a balance sheet of mid-twentieth-century trends in design.*
1953 Travels to Brazil as a member of the São Paolo jury, continues on to Peru and then the US. Lectures at the Design Conference in Aspen, Colorado. Bill takes third place in the international sculpture competition for a "Monument to an Unknown Political Prisoner."
1953/1954 Project for an architectural tender for the Freudenberg cantonal school in Zurich.
1955 Max Bill edits the 4th edition of Wassily Kandinsky's book *Punkt und Linie zur Fläche* (with an introduction by himself) and the Milan publication *Ludwig Mies van der Rohe.* Project for a monument to Georg Büchner in Darmstadt.
1956 Plans and builds the City of Ulm pavilion at the Baden-Württemberg state exhibition of trade and industry in Stuttgart (together with HfG teachers and students). Bill becomes a member of the German Werkbund. Designs first watch models for Junghans in Schramberg.

1956/1957 The Ulm Museum shows a large Max Bill retrospective that subsequently travels on to Munich, Duisburg, Hagen, and Zurich.
1957 Resigns from the governing board of the Ulm HfG following differences of opinion with the Geschwister Scholl Foundation and the governors. Plans and builds the Cinévox cinema complex with multistory apartment building in Neuhausen.
1958 A Festschrift to mark Max Bill's 50th birthday is published by Eugen Gomringer. Retrospective in museums in Leverkusen, Stuttgart, and Winterthur.
1959 Bill becomes a member of the Bund Schweizer Architekten (BSA).
1960 Organizes the exhibition konkrete kunst. 50 jahre entwicklung at the Helmhaus in Zurich. Organizes the exhibition *Dokumentation über Marcel Duchamp* at the Zurich Kunstgewerbemuseum and is editor of the catalog. Bill becomes a member of the Swiss Art Commission.
1960–1961 Plans and builds the Fleckhaus and Bold houses in Odenthal-Erberich, just outside Cologne.
Plans and builds the administrative offices of Imbau-Spannbeton AG in Leverkusen. Plans and builds the workshop building for Lichtdruck AG in Dielsdorf.
1961–1964 Conception and construction of the "Bilden und Gestalten" sector at Expo 64 in Lausanne.
1961–1968 Member of the City of Zurich parliament.
1964 Bill is made an honorary member of the American Institute of Architects (AIA).
1964–1974 Extension and remodelling of the Radio Zurich studios, together with Willy Roost.
1965 Construction and interior design of the theater tent on Zurich's Lindenhof for a production of *Ubu Roi* by Alfred Jarry.
1966/1967 Plans and builds the Lavoitobel bridge in Tamins, in collaboration with the engineering offices of Rôs, Aschwanden & Speck.
1966–1968 Designs and builds his own house and studio in Zumikon.
1967 His sculpture *windsäule* (wind column) is presented in front of the Swiss Pavilion at the International and Universal Exposition in Montreal.
1967–1971 Bill becomes a member of the Swiss Federal Parliament. He is given a chair in Environmental Design at the Hochschule für bildende Künste, Hamburg.
1968 City of Zurich Art Prize. Talk on the subject of "Das Behagen im Kleinstaat" ("Small-town contentment"). Builds the first *pavillonskulptur* at the Hakone Open-Air Museum in Kanagawa Prefecture, Japan.
1971–1975 Bill makes several trips to the US. Prepares a large retrospect, which is shown at the Albright-Knox Art Gallery in Buffalo, the Los Angeles County Museum of Art, and the San Francisco Museum of Art.
1972 Becomes a member of the Akademie der Künste, Berlin.
1976 Special "max bill" issue of the magazine *du*.
1979/80 Prepares the travelling retrospective *Georges Vantongerloo* with stops in Washington, Dallas, and Los Angeles.
1979–1983 Builds the *pavilion sculpture* in Zurich's Bahnhofstrasse. Albert Einstein monument in Ulm.
1980 Max Bill is awarded the Grand Cross of Merit by the Federal Republic of Germany and an honorary doctorate from the City of Stuttgart.
1982 Awarded the Kaiserring by the City of Goslar and the Belgian Order of the Crown and is a made a corresponding member of the Académie d'Architecture in Paris. Commissioned by the Deutsche Bank to produce a new version of his sculpture *kontinuität*.
1983 Designs the play *Beruf: Arlecchino* for the Zurich Opera Factory. The City of Zurich organizes the exhibition *max bill* at the Helmhaus to mark the artist's 75th birthday. Made a Commandeur des Arts et Lettres in France.
1985–1994 Chairman of the Bauhaus-Archiv in Berlin.
1986 Elected vice president of the Berlin Akademie der Künste. Completes the new version of *kontinuität* in Frankfurt am Main.
1987 Retrospectives in Weimar, Prague, and Frankfurt.
1988 Death of Binia Bill.
1991 Marries the art historian Angela Thomas.
1993 Awarded the Praemium Imperiale in Japan and made a Chevalier de la Légion d'honneur, France.
1994 Max Bill receives an honorary doctorate from the Eidgenössische Technische Hochschule Zürich (Swiss Federal Institute of Technology). He dies on December 9 during a trip to Berlin.

**Max Bill's
View of Things**

Edited by Lars Müller
Coordination: Rebekka Kiesewetter
Copyediting: Keonaona Peterson, Laura McLardy
Proofreading: Danko Szabo
Translation: Jennifer Taylor, Karen Williams (Ger–Eng)
Design: Lars Müller
Production: Integral Lars Müller / Esther Butterworth and Martina Mullis
Paper: Hello Fat Matt, 1.1, 135 g/m^2
Printing and binding: Kösel, Altusried-Krugzell, Germany

© 2015 Lars Müller Publishers; max, binia + jakob bill foundation, Adligenswil / ProLitteris, Zurich; Foundation Ernst Scheidegger Archive, Zurich, and the authors

Credits:
© max, binia + jakob bill foundation, Adligenswil / ProLitteris, Zurich, for all works by Max Bill
© max, binia + jakob bill foundation, Adligenswil, for all texts, written by Max Bill
© Foundation Ernst Scheidegger Archive, Zurich, for all photographs by Ernst Scheidegger: pp. 5, 31, 33, 34/35, 36/37.

No part of this book may be used or reproduced in any form or manner whatsoever without prior written permission, except in the case of brief quotations embodied in critical articles and reviews.

Lars Müller Publishers
Zürich, Switzerland
www.lars-mueller-publishers.com

ISBN 978-3-03778-372-6

Printed in Germany

Acknowledgments

The editor and publisher wish to thank all those who have contributed to the success of this publication. Particular thanks go to Chantal Bill for the care with which she accompanied the project. The Museum für Gestaltung, Zurich / Design Collection, the Foundation Ernst Scheidegger Archive, and the max, binia + jakob bill foundation provided the visual material and granted access to the textual sources. The publication of this book in its present form was made possible with the generous support of

Swiss Arts Council Pro Helvetia

Fachstelle Kultur Kanton Zürich

Stadt Zürich Kultur

Ernst Göhner Stiftung

max, binia + jakob bill stiftung